SILVER BULLS

SILVER BULLS

*

by

PAUL SARNOFF

ARLINGTON HOUSE PUBLISHERS

Westport, Connecticut

For my beloved grandson Mark

Library of Congress Cataloging in Publication Data

Sarnoff, Paul.
  Silver bulls.

  Includes index.
  1. Silver. I. Title.
HG305.S24   332.64'5   80-23614
ISBN 0-87000-480-8

MANUFACTURED IN THE UNITED STATES OF AMERICA

9 8 7 6 5 4 3 2

*

CONTENTS

. . ."In a society such as ours, where ideas are supposed to prove their value by free and open conflict, it is the duty and function of individuals to project their points of view so long as they act responsibly and with due regard for the rights of others . . ."

MORRIS I. ERNST,
Censorship.

BY WAY OF EXPLANATION:

The first four chapters of this book have been fictionalized to present a simple introduction to various facets of a highly complex international market. Chapters 5 through 8 represent my version of the widely publicized "Silver Situation" occurring between August 31, 1979, and March 31, 1980. The events described in this book are based upon the public record of silver trading activities as reported by the CFTC, the Commodities Exchange, Inc., the Chicago Board of Trade, media publications, and the record of legislative hearings before the Congress. Chapter 9 is a brief explanation of major silver trading strategies; and chapter 10 reflects my outlook on silver's future. Material for this book has been obtained from sources deemed reliable, but accuracy is not guaranteed.

I also want it clearly understood that the opinions expressed and the conclusions reached are entirely my own, and are not to be construed as reflecting either the opinions or the conclusions of the management of the company I worked for during manuscript preparation or of its parent company.

Therefore, any sins of commission or omission are strictly my own. With this in mind, I sincerely hope you enjoy the book.

PAUL SARNOFF
Oceanside, New York
August 25, 1980

*

ONE

*

THE
SILVER
LONGS

At precisely five on the morning of October 18, 1979, the world's second largest silver long rolled out of bed, shaved, showered, devoured the *New York Times* with breakfast—and made a succession of brief phone calls, some of them across the Atlantic. After scribbling quick calculations on the back of an envelope, he hurried out to his Jaguar, waiting in the driveway of his modest northern New Jersey home. Deftly he turned the ignition key and automatically switched on the CB. Even before the transmitter began its interminable crackle, the car leaped like an unleashed tiger down the driveway toward the parkway leading to the George Washington Bridge.

As the twelve-cylinder motor purred its song of power, a single sentence echoed repeatedly through this silver bull's mind: "I can't believe how much money I'm making . . . I can't believe how much money I'm making. . . ."

For more than twenty years, Norton Waltuch, this silver long, had been patiently perfecting the tools of his trade, taming the pits. A member of nearly all major futures exchanges, he had carefully constructed the reputation of being a shade shrewder than most traders who made their living from price changes. He had also acquired the capability of being seconds quicker than most traders in both order entry and order execution. Moreover, the media, especially the *Wall Street Journal,* had greatly enhanced his reputation by reporting that his mere appearance on the exchange floor actually caused the price of silver to soar.

Trading in the silver pits in New York and Chicago has always required nerves of steel and platinum balls. This New Jersey silver bull happened to have a goodly supply of both. And now, as he worked his car through traffic on his way to the World Trade Center, the world's second leading silver long realized that his main chance to make many millions had finally arrived. In past years there had been missed chances for fortunes trading cocoa, coffee, sugar, orange juice. But none of these agricultural commodities could compare with the profit possibility now building in silver.

Several hours later on that same October morning, in Dallas, Texas, the world's largest silver long gazed at a slip of paper lying on his desk. Nelson Bunker Hunt, inheritor of one of the world's great oil fortunes, was no stranger to big money. But even he could not suppress a thrill of excitement at the numbers on the paper.

While the prices of gold and silver often move together, the price-setting mechanism is different for the two metals. The most popularly quoted price for gold is the London fix, set twice each trading day by five members of the London Gold Market, meeting in the offices of N. M. Rothschild. Three of those five traders then gather at Mocatta & Goldsmid to fix the price of silver. The ritual for silver is performed only once a day.

Trading in New York and Chicago goes on hours after the London markets have closed, and prices can move up or down in response to market developments and shifting sentiment, but the London fixes for gold and silver normally set guidelines each day for all the other precious metals market in the world.

In 1973 Bunker Hunt, along with his two brothers and numerous friends, began stockpiling silver in all its marketable forms: bars, ingots, scrap silver, coins, and contracts for future delivery. His passion for the metal paralleled Baron von Thyssen's compulsion to acquire old master paintings. In both cases the mania went beyond the urge to amass ever larger fortunes. Hunt, it was said, possessed a mystical feeling for silver, a sense of its worth not only as a financial asset but as a strategic natural resource destined to become dangerously rare in the industrialized world.

Since 1946 the industrialized nations of the world have consumed more silver than they have mined, to meet growing demand for silver bullion, jewelry, coins, and ornamental objects. As the Soviet Union and the People's Republic of China become more westernized, their need for silver will explode; and it is only a matter of time before there will be an invisible war between the forces of capitalism and those of communism for adequate supplies of silver.

Bunker Hunt is a man who believes in the virtues of free enterprise, in the right of men to take business risks and to enjoy the rewards of their success. He believes in the right of men to choose their associates and to avoid the presence of those with whom they do not choose to associate. Bunker Hunt and his associates, on this October day, were enjoying the fruit of their risk taking, and of their association in a highly profitable joint enterprise.

The rising price of silver poured a growing stream of cash and equity into his personal accounts in the U.S. and abroad. Part of this stream was generated by commodity futures trading rules that require daily settlements by winners and losers as the market fluctuates. Shorts who have sold silver they do not own in the hope of buying more cheaply later must pay "variation margin" to guarantee the veracity of the contracts if the market rises instead of falling. Longs, of course, face a similar demand when prices fall. Thus, those who judge the market correctly are rewarded in added cash at the close of every trading day.

As a silver long, holding vast amounts of physical silver as well as futures contracts, Bunker Hunt found himself the recipient of millions in extra equity as the market rose. Those millions could be put to instant use to invest in securities, real estate—and even to buy a sizable stake in an internationally famous stock brokerage company—all without paying any interest for the flow of funds from the brokers and banks holding his silver accounts.

As Bunker Hunt considered how best to use the many millions of interest-free dollars pouring into his accounts each trading day, he recalled a recent TV guest appearance when the host insensitively asked: "Just how much silver do you really have?"

And he chuckled inwardly as he answered: "Only God and I know; and God ain't talking. So neither am I."

In Sao Paulo, Brazil, in the afternoon of that same October day, the world's third largest silver bull sat studying his current position. Naji Robert Nahas, a Lebanese, ruled twenty-three multinational corporations involved in diverse activities, from steamships to racehorses. All at once he recalled buying six mares for $400,000 in Chile. He smiled to himself as he reflected that though the Dallas silver bulls may possess more silver, they didn't get as good a horse trade at the same auction because they paid almost $300,000 for only two horses.

Like the Dallas investors, Nahas had become enamored of the metal that someone once called "the poor man's gold," and decided to stockpile silver futures and physicals to hedge himself from being ruined by the oil-fed inflation that ran rampant in both Brazil and the United States.

Gold, of course, has been a traditional hedge against inflation. While gold in 1978 had risen by 37 percent, silver had advanced by only 27 percent. Nahas believed that silver would now appreciate at a faster rate than gold.

After examining his positions, the silver long from Brazil called his broker in New York to buy more silver.

On the side of a hill in a park in downtown Geneva the hands of an enormous floral clock indicate the time by their passing of clusters of growing flowers. In October the time in Geneva is five hours later than New York's Eastern Daylight Time.

On the evening of October 18, 1979, a group of Arabs attended a dinner party in the beautifully appointed Orangerie at La Perl du Lac. But the participants at this soirée hardly noticed the wild duck, cooked in a memorable sauce. Nor did they rave about the savor of the perfectly served Vâcheron cheese and expresso. The main topic of conversation for these silver longs was, of course, silver—its present price and where it could possibly be heading by Christmas . . .

Silver Valley, Idaho, is about twenty-four miles long and four miles wide. Here in the Coeur d'Alene district are the world's richest silver mines. While most of the silver mined elsewhere in the world is a by-product of other ores, the silver in the Idaho mines is primary ore. That is, silver is the principal product, other metals secondary.

On that October morning, Phil Lindstrom, investment manager for Hecla Mining Company, one of North America's largest and most famous silver mines, suddenly looked intently at his watch. Wallace, Idaho, time is three hours earlier than New York, and, to say the least, Idaho's silver bull has had to rise rather early for the past thirty-eight years to monitor the world's silver markets.

But on this October day the Idaho silver long, who owned silver bullion, silver coins, silver futures, not to mention a sizable chunk of stock in his silver company, picked up the phone and began calling friendly analysts all over the country. His message to these researchers covered the concept that every rise in the silver price brought increased earnings to his company and for the shareholders. "So as silver goes up in price," he noted, "We're mining money."

In Riyadh, the capital of Saudi Arabia, that same October afternoon, Mahmoud Fustok, his country's leading silver bull and business counselor for certain of Saudi Arabia's prominent families, concluded that silver was heading in only one direction—up. He recalled that certain members of the royal family to whom he was rather close had been criticized in the past for gambling at Monte Carlo. Fustok preferred to make discreet investments in a natural asset that seemed almost a sure thing. "We cannot invest in interest-bearing obligations," he explained to one of his New York investment advisers who failed to understand the nuances of the Moslem view of usury. Then Fustok added, "But we can and do invest risk capital in order to seek profits."

And so he ordered increased purchases of silver futures, because in October 1979 silver seemed like a better bet than anything on the tables at Monte Carlo.

On that same October day, Louisiana's leading silver bull, James Blanchard, completed arrangements for his annual New Orleans conference on money and metals. Called "New Orleans '79," this conference in early November would draw more than 3,200 attendees, who would pay almost $400 each, plus their travel and living expenses, to hear Jim Blan-

6

chard's hard money message. In previous years gold had been the focus of interest. But in 1979 the leading issue was silver. The reason was that in 1979 the price of silver had tripled, outpacing gold, which had not quite doubled in price.

The silver attraction at that time was such that the host of the conference offered a Canadian silver dollar (then worth about $12) in exchange for a free ticket to the banquet that came with payment of the tuition for the conference. Not so oddly, many of the ticket holders turned in their paper Annie Oakleys for the shiny silver coins. It turned out that within three months those who did would be able to resell their coins for almost five times their value at the time of exchange.

October generally lays at least one hard frost on certain sections of New England. But this October 18 was a warm and sunny Indian summer day in Newtown, Conn., where James Blakely was putting the finishing touches to a new issue of his *Silver and Gold Report*.

Blakely's subscribers, numbering 30,000 in the U.S. and abroad, knew that this silver bull was also a silver long, who had run a $10,000 stake into more than $250,000 by trading silver futures. He not only had confidence in the metal, but he believed that his subscribers would continue to earn profits by following the advice that he gave them in his semi-monthly newsletter.

His current issue ready to go, he started preparing for his journey to New Orleans, where he would set up a marketing booth at Jim Blanchard's conference, attract new subscribers, and create new silver longs and silver bulls.

Indeed, October 1979 became the month that silver longs and silver bulls around the world would long remember. At that time limitless pocketbooks were opening up all over the world to buy, hold, and stockpile physical silver and to acquire futures contracts.

Traditionally, silver longs—holders of contracts to buy for future delivery—had rarely exercised their options to demand delivery of physical metal. Rather, 97 percent to 99 percent of all contracts had been settled by their sale at prices keyed to the current value of silver. But that October it became startlingly clear that several of the largest silver longs intended to invoke the letter of their legal rights and demand delivery of fine metal, in 1,000-ounce bars 99.9 percent pure, as delivery, and apparently there was not enough fine silver in storage to meet such demands. If this were to occur during December and March (the next delivery months), a silver squeeze could be a pregnant possibility, if not an actual reality.

So while the longs in silver enjoyed the increase each trading day in the equity in their positions, the shorts in silver grew increasingly distressed—if not actually alarmed.

*

TWO

*

THE SILVER SHORTS

Webster's Collegiate Dictionary provides eleven definitions for the adjective "short," but the one germane to the commodity business and the security business is number eleven. The definition goes, in part . . . "not having goods or property that one has sold in anticipation of a fall in prices."

Unlike transactions on stock exchanges, where shares in corporations are bought and sold, futures exchanges deal only in contracts to receive or deliver specific lots of commodities on a specified date in the future. The contracts are standard, varying only in price and delivery date. The clearinghouse of the exchange guarantees that the contracting parties—the buyer and the seller—will meet their obligations. In effect, then, a futures speculator does not buy or sell short a commodity; he contracts to buy or sell the commodity at a future date, at an agreed price, no matter whether the market for the spot or cash commodity rises or falls in the meantime.

Because the prices of cash commodities are often volatile, the holders of long contracts (contracts to buy or receive) and the holders of short contracts (to sell or deliver) find that the value of their contracts changes frequently. Clearinghouse accounts are squared, or settled, every day, by money flowing through the clearinghouse from the member with adverse positions to the members with favorable positions.

In the case of silver, the standard Comex contract calls for delivery of 5,000 ounces of silver 99.9 percent pure, or .999 fine (triple nine, in the jargon of the market). If a commission house, that is, a broker acting as an agent for public speculators or commercial hedgers and a clearing member, is on a net basis short 1,000 silver contracts on the New York Commodities Exchange (Comex) or Chicago Board of Trade (CBOT), the firm is responsible for 5,000,000 ounces (1,000 contracts of 5,000 ounces each), and so is liable for depositing $5 million for every dollar of rise in the market price of the involved contracts. Although in theory the clearing member acting for customers will promptly collect any adverse margins (the professional term is variation margin) from the client, the clearinghouse holds the broker member responsible and will collect the money immediately, whether or not the member has been able to collect from the customers. That is why a clearing member with sizable client positions in futures either long or short constantly suffers exposure.

By October 18, 1979, it was clear that Comex and CBOT members who had net long positions held by the silver bulls had little cause for concern about exposure. Silver had just about tripled in price since the beginning of the year, a highly favorable development for the longs.

Conversely, the commodity exchanges were becoming increasingly concerned with the exposure of the shorts in silver; but oddly enough, they were busying themselves with the affairs of the longs. In retrospect, this was understandable, because most of the market speculators who had gone short silver had already been wiped out or had liquidated their short positions with offsetting contracts at severe losses. These traders had misread the market. Noting silver's long rise since the first of the year, they concluded it was ripe for a fall. As the error of their judgment became clear, they dropped out, absorbing their losses. So who were the shorts still active in the market in October and the months to follow?

The shorts had to be (a) commercial producers of silver using the futures market to hedge or shift their risk to speculators who simply hoped for a quick trading profit, and (b) a handful of bullion dealers, who were professional buyers and sellers of precious metals.

Commercial producers are the companies that mine and refine the physical metal. Since the contracts for future delivery generally command a higher price than the cash or spot market, and since the producer must insure sale of his product through each month of the year, he sells the metal forward in the form of future contracts. When the metal is actually refined, it can be sold at the going price.

If this price is lower than the futures contract price, the producer can congratulate himself on having insured against the price drop. He sells his newly refined metal at the low market price, but takes a profit on his futures short sale by covering the contract at a much lower purchase price. If the price of spot metal has risen, the producer collects the higher price for his physical metal, but takes a loss on covering his short contracts. By hedging, he has avoided speculative risk or exposure, in the interest of assuring a profitable price for his product.

Bullion dealers also use the futures exchanges to hedge metal they hold in inventory against possible price declines. To do this they presell some of the metal they expect to receive from the recycling of scrap, or from other sources. Bullion dealers realize income from the difference in price between the scrap they buy continuously and the silver they sell to actual users, such as flatware manufacturers, photography suppliers, and other industrial consumers.

Since bullion dealers traditionally buy in the spot or cash market, finance their purchases through bank loans, and go short on futures exchanges at prices higher than they have paid for the metal, they fill a position on the futures exchanges something like that of specialists on the New York Stock Exchange, who are obliged to make a market for their stocks no matter how violent price swings. These bullion dealers are constantly in the market, supplying short contracts to long buyers, even with the speculating public has deserted the short side of the market.

There is little doubt that by mid-October the major shorts on the silver exchanges were the bullion dealers, who were marking up the price of silver futures to meet the increasing demands of the silver bulls. Of course they had to accomplish this without risking excessive exposure. Therefore, the bullion dealers increased their purchases of metal, scrap, and ores, at the same time hedging by selling contracts short at successively higher prices at the Comex and CBOT.

Since they supposedly were hedged, it should not have mattered to the bullion dealers whether the price of silver rose or fell. But while most of the dealers religiously covered any exposure by selling (going short) silver, they faced the obligation of meeting daily variation margin calls, that is, depositing cash with the clearinghouses to cover their liabilities. This was bothersome and expensive.

By October some of the bullion dealers were putting up many millions of dollars in variation margin to the exchanges every day. This did not involve serious difficulty for most of the dealers, since the value of the metal they held was rising with the market, and they were able to use these stocks of metal as collateral for bank loans to meet the variation margins.

On the October morning when the New Jersey bull drove his Jaguar at demonic speed toward New York and a rendezvous with the silver market, a limousine wheeled up a long driveway leading to the unique oaken door of a baronial mansion in Harrison, New York. A tall psychiatrist, impeccably dressed, his thick glasses askew, dashed out the door and into the waiting car. Wordlessly, the chauffeur slipped the car into gear and smoothly completed the circle of a driveway as long as an athletic field track. Then, carefully emerging from a narrow road called Timber Trail, the limousine turned right and headed for the Hutchinson River Parkway toward New York. As the miles unrolled on the trip to his office at the World Trade Center, that doctor, who is chairman of what publicists modestly call "the world's largest bullion dealer," kept mumbling over and over: "How can we stop this? . . . How can we stop this?"

October in Lima, Peru, signals the end of the *garua,* the period from June to October when the sun rarely shines. During these months the city of Lima is often blanketed by a weird inversion. The result is that the sun is hardly ever seen because of the blanket of clouds overhanging the city.

On October 18 Alfredo Fonseca, the hedge-meister of Peru's mineral marketing agency, examined the position of his "company" at commodity brokers in the United States and Britain. He was responsible for making the trading decisions that would protect the agency from market risks. And since the agency is charged with the purchase of concentrated silver ore and other ores from major mining interests of Peru, it was natural that its trading position at the brokerage houses was predominantly short.

In the normal conduct of its business the agency purchases and pays for the newly mined ore concentrate, then ships the crude product to Mexico, where it is refined into salable metal. Some five or six months after buying the concentrate, the agency sells the finished metal at the going market price. To protect the agency from adverse market developments—a fall in the price of silver during the time it is in the possession of the agency—the hedge-meister sells futures contracts for forward delivery. If the price of silver falls, the company is protected against loss.

But silver had already advanced almost 300 percent in less than ten months, and the temptation was to overhedge, that is, to sell short more contracts than those needed for protection. The hedge-meister had been advised by Merrill Lynch and E. F. Hutton, with whom he maintained active accounts, that the price of silver was due for a fall. Alfredo Fonseca picked up a telephone and called the giant American wire houses where he conducts his hedging business, and discussed going short some more silver.

In the world of great corporations, there is a legendary doctor named Armand Hammer, who with consummate skill has managed to do business profitably with both the Communist and Western worlds. While the central corporation of his empire is known as Occidental Petroleum, its subsidiary interests extend into other natural resource companies producing, among other things, gold and silver ore.

On the morning of October 18, 1979, Dr. Hammer instructed his subordinates to stop hedging in silver. "Something is happening in the silver market," he decided, and added, "Better wait until the price is much higher before going short."

In Washington, D.C., the world's greatest silver bear heads a lobbying agency supported by the industries who use large quantities of silver. The interest of these members lies in maintaining an abundant supply of silver at the lowest possible price. Walter Frankland, gray-haired, scholarly, distinguished in bearing and appearance, for many years has used his ability, his impressive fund of information, and his countless friends in Washington to influence the government to sell its stockpiled silver at low prices. His silver-using clients are the natural beneficiaries of this influence.

In 1977 Walter Frankland mounted an intensive campaign to persuade Congress to dispose of the 139.5 million ounces of silver remaining in a stockpile that once contained 2 billion ounces. The "surplus" had been sold off at prices ranging from $1.29 to $2.50 an ounce. But although his objective had been aided by Congressmen and agency aides alike, the rest of the silver stockpile had never been sold.

On October 18, 1979, he was set to make another try. A bill had been drafted that would have opened the way to disposal of the remaining stockpile. An early version of the bill called for the sale of 60 million ounces. After objections were raised by such silver-bull Congressmen as Larry Mc-Donald of Georgia and Steve Symms of Idaho, the amount was reduced to 15 million ounces, and, finally, to 5 million ounces. "We have got to get this bill passed," he muttered, "the price of silver is already so high users are going to grumble and stop buying. Maybe a silver squeeze is developing. . . ."

He dialed a local commodity brokerage office to learn the latest Comex price for silver.

Indeed, October 1979 turned out to be a distressing time for the major silver shorts and the die-hard silver bears. It also became the month in which the price of silver made a base that would carry it later to heights never before experienced.

Meanwhile, the shorts had to pony up millions in variation margins each time silver made an advance.

*

THREE

*

THE SILVER REGULATORS

The pagoda in Sri Lanka stands on a five hundred-square-foot—seven inches thick—foundation of solid silver. The ancient architect's choice of silver as a construction material in this case rests on the belief that silver brings luck. But the commissioners of the federal agency responsible for protecting the public in commodity futures transactions realize that prices are not made by luck; they are made by people.

For many years the commodity exchanges operated virtually free of federal regulation. The exchanges are private membership corporations, controlled by boards of directors dominated by the professionals using the exchanges—the floor brokers, commission houses, and bullion dealers. A minority of directors was appointed to represent the public. The exchanges have always been virtually a law to themselves.

17

That all changed with the creation of the Commodity Futures Exchange Commission in 1975 to regulate commodity trading. Aside from bringing rules to a previously unregulated business, the legislation contained another unusual feature. The CFTC it created was a "sunshine" agency, scheduled to self-destruct unless Congress renewed its basic authorization. In 1978 Congress extended the CFTC's life to 1982.

The key purpose of the CFTC is "to detect threats of corners, manipulations, or other major market disturbances." Ironically, the legislation does not define manipulation or corner. But the CFTC staff evaluates the elements of manipulation to be:

1. A trader or group of traders acting in concert to establish the capacity to affect the price of a commodity.
2. The exercise of that capacity to affect a price.
3. Creation of an artificial price.
4. Intent to affect that price.

Under provisions of the Commodity Exchange Act it is a felony to manipulate or attempt to manipulate the price of any commodity in either the cash or futures markets. Penalties range up to a fine of $100,000 or five years in prison, or both.

The detection of possible market manipulation is one of the major tasks of the CFTC. By receiving and analyzing the records of the exchanges, and sometimes running the records through elaborate computer programs, the staff looks for evidence of market manipulation. These sophisticated searches are designed to turn up any of four patterns that suggest manipulation:

1. By analyzing the positions held by traders in future contracts and physical commodities, and comparing these positions with the total available supply, the CFTC can de-

termine if a trader or a group of traders working together have the ability to influence a commodity price.

2. The staff monitors large positions daily to determine whether actions taken by large traders actually affect the price. These actions may include the taking of new positions, either long or short, or roll overs, meaning liquidating contracts for near-term deliveries in favor of new positions in more distant months.

3. To determine whether an "artificial price" is being created, the staff economists conduct daily reviews of cash commodity prices and their relationship with future prices.

4. The fourth ingredient of manipulation—intent—cannot be precisely monitored. But conclusions may be drawn from information the traders provide to the Commission, and from the trader's past and present actions in the market.

By October 1979 the CFTC had expanded to more than five hundred employees, led by four commissioners, who served by Presidential appointment with Senate confirmation. One seat on the five-member Commission was vacant.

About the most charitable thing that could be said about the Commission was that in its short life it had failed to win the confidence of the professional traders it was supposed to regulate. In protecting the public against fraud, it was about as effective as the Administration's anti-inflation program.

A major problem lay with the leadership. The first chairman, appointed by President Nixon, was William T. Bagley, a Washington lawyer with a taste for seeing his name in headlines. Soon after the Commision began operating in 1975 this impartial referee was quoted as declaring, "all the New York Exchanges should be closed up."

The Commission's vice-chairman, John Rainbolt, was responsible for implementing a Congressional directive to create an exchange-traded market in commodity options.* During the first five years of the agency's operation, he made four trips to London to learn how the responsible and effective British system for options trading works. On his twenty-second fact-finding trip he explained why the CFTC intended to ban those options "to protect the public."

Despite the CFTC's shaky beginning, Congress extended its life in 1978 for four more years. However, President Carter did not reappoint the chairman and vice-chairman, and they returned to the private practice of law.

Acting with uncharacteristic speed, President Carter soon appointed a new chairman, a Harvard-trained economist, James Stone, then only thirty-one. As insurance commissioner for Massachusetts, Stone had instituted a number of reforms in the regulation of the insurance industry. His appointment brought the strength of the Commission up to four; the fifth seat is still unfilled at this writing, and may remain empty until after the 1980 Presidential election.

In office, the new CFTC chairman liked to conduct his business against a background of classical music, and after greeting a visitor, would place a Mozart record on the turntable before getting down to the business at hand. But even Mozart was of little solace to a man responsible for regulating the commodity trading industry at a time when its very foundations were being threatened by the gathering crisis in silver. Under pressure, Stone became visibly strained, and took medical leave for six weeks, returning on October 12. The responsibility for monitoring the silver situation fell to another commissioner, Read Dunn, a mature, methodical investigator.

Dunn was worried about the pattern he saw developing in

---

*An option is the right, but not the obligation, to buy or sell a given commodity at a given price, up to the date of expiration. A futures contract obliges the buyer to buy and the seller to sell a commodity on a set date unless an offsetting contract is concluded in the meantime.

the silver market. Some of the silver longs, as their contracts approached maturity, were refusing to sell offsetting contracts, but instead were giving notice that they intended to take delivery of the metal. This was entirely legal, but it was a major reversal of past practice, in which the futures market had served a hedging function, not as a market for physical metal. In the past, fewer than 3 percent of the contracts had been settled by actual delivery of metal. The growing practice of demanding delivery could change the character of the market. It also put pressure on the shorts—the sellers—who were obligated to deliver physical metal. Silver was becoming alarmingly scarce under the market's relentless demand.

Dunn had another reason for concern. He saw that much of the silver being delivered was being flown out of the United States for storage in London and Switzerland. Much of the buying of silver futures came through Switzerland's Banque Populaire (Volksbank), prohibited under Swiss law from revealing the identity of its principals. Dunn suspected that some of the buying came from Communist sources, and he determined to use his powers to try to find out who was buying, how much, and why.

The commissioner best qualified by background and experience to direct the silver investigation was Robert Martin, a Nixon appointee who had served on the Commission from its creation. He had been a chairman of the Chicago Board of Trade and had broad experience in both the cash and futures markets. But because the Commission and the Carter Administration were sensitive to charges leveled against other regulatory bodies—that they had been captured by the industries they regulated—Martin's role in the silver investigation was severely limited. He attended meetings and received reports.

The newest commissioner, except for the chairman, was David Gartner, a Carter appointee, a man of demonstrated intestinal fortitude. Despite pressures and controversy that might have driven a weaker man from office, Gartner worked quietly behind the scenes to try to make the Commission's work effective and fair. He was less concerned with ferreting out market manipulation, whose existence he doubted, but was considerably concerned with the disappearance of silver from the U.S. and its possible movement into the hostile hands of Comecon powers. Other information suggested that this fear was well founded.

Gartner and the other commissioners were also concerned with certain transactions taking place outside the control of the commodities exchanges and the CFTC. One of these deals involved Mocatta Metals, the big bullion dealer, and a Bermuda-based corporation called IMIC. This offshore corporation was owned by Nelson Bunker Hunt, his brother W. Herbert Hunt, by another Hunt corporation based in Delaware, and by two Saudi Arabian money men said to represent the Saudi royal family. Their names were Ali Bin Mussalem and Sheik Mohammed Aboud Al Amoudi. The Mocatta-IMIC deal called for Mocatta to deliver to IMIC 23 million ounces of silver, an exchange for physicals (EFP) transaction that reduced IMIC's long position, and also reduced Mocatta's short position by 4,600 contracts.

Actually, this transaction, worth about $400 million, involved no silver deliverable on Comex, whose rules specify that delivery shall be made only in 1,000-ounce bars of triple nine metal (.999 fine). In this swap of open contracts for metal, Mocatta delivered bags of coins and European silver of lesser purity than Comex demands. The transaction reduced the daily variation margin that Mocatta had to pay. Some observers also guessed that Mocatta, big as it was, simply did not have enough triple nine silver to meet its contracts, and the word around the exchanges was that the Hunts had let Mocatta off the hook.

Commissioner Read Dunn, who was busily examining the silver situation from the standpoint of the longs, had scant time to bother about the condition of the shorts. Dunn was particularly interested in finding out the identity of the forty-five accounts at Banque Populaire in Switzerland who were buying plenty of silver and flying it out of the U.S.

In a report submitted in April 1980 to the Committee on Agriculture, Nutrition and Forestry of the U.S. Senate, the Commission stated:

> In late September and early October it became apparent that IMIC [the Hunt-Saudi connection] and a few of the Conti accounts [those managed and advised by the leading Swiss silver bull, Tom Waldeck] intended to accept delivery on their long futures positions. In September 1979, IMIC accepted delivery of 1,184 futures contracts (5,920,000 ounces) in the Comex September future. Banque Populaire also took delivery of 915 contracts (4,575,000 ounces) and Nahas [the Sao Paulo silver bull] accepted 550 contracts (2,750,000 ounces) on that future. IMIC and Banque Populaire also took additional deliveries in October, IMIC accepting 1,344 contracts (6,720,000 ounces) on the CBOT [Board of Trade in Chicago] October future while Banque Populaire accepted 792 contracts (3,960,000 ounces) on the lightly traded Comex October future . . ."

During this period IMIC also effected another EFP with Sharps, Pixley for an additional 4 million ounces of silver (eight hundred contacts), thereby reducing IMIC's long futures position and Sharps, Pixley's costly shorts on Comex.

As the storm gathered over the silver markets that October, the public watchdog, CFTC, was both concerned and active, but it was content merely to continue its surveillance. The chairman, James Stone, considered taking a trip to London and one to China because of overwork. Read Dunn, the commissioner in charge of the silver investigation, tried to learn who the silver bulls were and what were their motives. The other two commissioners, Robert Martin and David Gartner, less involved in the moment-to-moment developments, began to worry about the condition of the shorts— the firms and individuals obligated to deliver massive amounts of silver that they might not possess. But at no time during that period did the CFTC conclude that any person, persons, or group was actually manipulating silver or causing the price to rise artificially.

Although the CFTC contended there was no manipulation of silver, this was not the sentiment among the boards of directors of Comex and CBOT.

*

FOUR

*

THE
SILVER
EXCHANGES

Silver futures contracts began trading on the New York Comex in 1963 and on the Chicago Board of Trade in 1969. Trading in these contracts occurs in areas designated on the exchange floors as "silver pits." The silver pits are concentric circles, resembling the waves made on the surface of a calm lake when a stone is dropped into the water. The inner circle or ring is at the lowest level, and steps rise from the inner circle to successively larger rings. The near month is traded inside; the further-out deliveries are traded on the steps of the pit. In general, every transaction in the pits occurs by public outcry. But the rules also permit longs and shorts to enter into EFP transactions (exchange of futures for physicals).

In such a transaction, the holder of the long contract becomes a buyer of the silver in physical form and the seller of his futures position. The opposite party, the short, becomes the buyer of the long futures contract and the seller of the physical silver.

Such a transaction does not have to be done at public outcry, but after it is completed, the transaction must be reported to the exchange floor committee, entered in the official records of the exchange, and announced, printed, and posted as an EFP.

If the exchange were a publicly operated agency, it is obvious that its rules would favor no special trading groups; rather, it would be designed to be fair and without favor to the longs or the shorts, the hedgers or the speculators.

But the Comex and the Chicago Board of Trade are *not* publicly owned institutions. They are organizations created to provide privileged trading arenas for members who pay large amounts of money for "seats." Rules governing the exchanges are proposed by exchange committees and adopted or rejected by the boards of directors. And the rules supposedly have always been designed to protect the soundness of the contracts made by the members and issued by the clearinghouses affiliated with the exchanges.

Unlike the CBOT, the Comex does not trade in agricultural products or their futures, only in the futures of metals and financial instruments. Until April 1975 the Comex was an authority unto itself. Members were bound to abide by the rules and regulations decreed by the exchange directors, but were not subject to regulation by the federal government. In a word, then, the Comex was an "unregulated exchange" where "unregulated commodity futures" were traded.

But after the CFTC came alive in 1975 things began to change at the Comex, now no longer an unregulated exchange trading unregulated futures contracts. Although the hand of regulation was light in many areas of exchange operations, the Comex now had to contend with federal supervision, regulation, and oversight.

It is natural that at Comex the board of directors should

represent the various interests and publics the institution serves. Board members include representatives of users and producers of metals and the bullion houses (the trade), floor brokers (the locals), and commission houses (registered futures commission merchants, or FCM's). In recent years Comex has expanded its board to include also "outside" directors from the world of industry, their purpose being to increase the fairness and objectivity of board decisions.

Trading volume on the Comex has increased at a stunning rate, leading its publicists to refer to the institution as "the world's largest metals exchange." This is inaccurate; Comex trades no metals, only contracts to buy and sell metals at some future date. In any case, its growth has resulted in large part from the "floor broker mentality" of many of its traders, a willingness to get in and out of the market for small profits or losses. This is facilitated by exchange rules that allow day trading—opening and closing of trades on the same day—without any margin at all.

By way of explanation, we might proceed down to the silver pit on the New York CEC (Commodity Exchange Center) on the eighth floor of No. 4 World Trade Center, in Lower Manhattan.

A visitor to the gallery on the ninth floor faces a vast open space two stories high and as big as a sports stadium. This huge room houses the combined trading facilities of the Comex, the New York Coffee, Sugar, and Cocoa Exchange, the New York Cotton Exchange, and the New York Mercantile Exchange. The combined exchange floor is the world's largest open room built without vertical supports. Workers on the floor often get the eerie feeling that the ceiling may at any moment fall on them. The traders, of course, are too busy to notice.

Viewed from the visitor's gallery, the silver pit on Comex occupies the cornermost three large pits allotted to the exchange. The silver pit is flanked by the gold pit and the copper pit. A fourth small pit, originally planned for options trading, is used for trading financial futures.

Various groups of people begin to form around the silver ring and on the steps shortly after 9:30 A.M. In the pit are Comex members who trade for their own account, members who trade as agents for other members, and Comex members who do both.

As the opening hour of 9:50 approaches, a rustle pervades the pits as members shuffle order tickets, index cards, even minicharts. Then, at ten-before-ten, all hell breaks loose. Shouting, screaming, hand-waving, finger-signaling, the silver traders frantically do their business. On the perimeter of the pits, clerks and messengers stand ready to rush reports of executions to the member booths, where the reports will be relayed by wire to brokerage houses, bullion houses, trade and commercial customers, and speculators all over the world.

On Comex, as at CBOT, there have always been trading limits. That is, by exchange rules, if the price for a future delivery rises or falls by a given amount, trading in that month is suspended. Only the current of "spot" month delivery operates without trading limits.

While the shouting, hand-waving, and finger signals may mystify the casual onlooker, they are full of meaning to floor denizens lurking in the pits. Among the knowledgeable onlookers are market monitors for leading brokerage firms; these observers report over hotlines to their offices precisely who is buying and selling. Comex members who trade for themselves may want to see the action in the pit before making their short-term, no-margin day trades. Other observers, who have nothing at all to do with the actual trading, may also be intensely interested in the action inside the pit.

It did not take a person with a Ph. D. degree in economics to realize that when the New Jersey silver bull, Norton Waltuch, or his floor brokers, entered the fray buying was about to flood the pits. And the locals (floor brokers who trade mostly for their own accounts) knew which way the market would go when Al Brodsky, acting for Bache, entered orders for the Dallas silver bull and his allies.

CFTC representatives are invariably stationed near the pits to see that the proprieties are observed, and wire service news reporters are there to report the action to the world. During 1979 and the spring of 1980 action in the silver pit surpassed anything previously recorded in the history of commodity trading.

In January 1979 a literate and observant reporter for the *Wall Street Journal,* covering the action in precious metals, noted: "Tight silver supplies have also sparked rumors of a possible market squeeze—the accumulation of a large number of contracts to force prices higher in the March delivery contract on the Commodity Exchange in New York."

"But, says ContiCommodity's Mr. Sarnoff, 'even though stocks are dropping pretty rapidly at the various exchanges there is still a lot of silver around.' . . ."

A few weeks later Dr. Henry Jarecki of Mocatta Metals was quoted in the same paper: "I think the severe supply shortage is becoming obvious. . . ." In the same column, the reporter wrote: "While most traders doubt that a squeeze will actually occur, they agree that the awareness of the possibility that the market can be squeezed is making them nervous and contributing to the price rise. . . ."

On April 27, 1979, silver stood at $7.58 an ounce, and Julie Salamon, the *Wall Street Journal* writer interested in precious metals, reported: "Paul Sarnoff . . . says, 'I'd buy silver currently because it's cheap relative to gold. . . .' "

All spring and into summer Julie Salamon followed the rocketing course of silver, and by September her headline went:

GOLD, SILVER PRICES UNFATHOMABLE
SURGE STIRRING RUMORS
OF BIG MONEY INVASION.

In the article, quoting opinions from diverse sources among the traders and regulators, she reported:

As often happens when prices move without any apparent reason, rumors of manipulation have filtered among traders and down to the Commodity Futures Trading Commission. . . . "We're monitoring the situation very closely," said John Manley, director of the CFTC's trading and markets division. He added that thus far the agency hasn't found a basis for the rumors and that "some of the economists here feel these prices are a very logical extension of world prices."

But what did the research director for the psychiatrist's bullion firm have to say? "Large precious metals dealers in New York, London, and Zurich, which normally play a dominant role in gold and silver markets, are all playing on the sidelines . . . (and) the recent price surge has been the cumulative effect of a lot of individuals buying gold and silver. . . ." The good doctor's spokesman failed, of course, to mention that if people were buying, somebody had to be selling—and the persons most anxious to do the business made the price.

It was also in her column of September 6, 1979, that Julie Salamon began to mention our New Jersey silver bull: " 'The recent fervent interest in precious metals on the part of wealthy individuals isn't surprising,' says Norton Waltuch . . . whose large purchases of silver have been instrumental in spurring prices skyward, traders say."

" 'Just look at the vast pools of money floating around the world,' says Mr. Waltuch. 'Paper currencies are declining. People who have it, have to put their money somewhere.' "

Rumors flooded the trading pit to the effect that the New Jersey silver bull now had a "limitless pocketbook" because he spearheaded the flow of Saudi Arabian oil money into silver.

On September 19 Ms. Salamon wrote:

Much of the demand for silver lately is widely believed to have come from Norton Waltuch, a veteran commodity trader who is a Comex member. . . . Mr. Waltuch, who has amassed a very large long position, or commitment to receive silver on behalf of unidentified clients, is cited by many traders as the

igniting force in the current round of spiraling prices. . . .
Last week his mere appearance on the floor of the Comex was
said to have sent silver prices as much as 30¢ an ounce higher.

Indeed, in September 1979 a rise of 30 cents was quite a
massive move for the once stable metal. By October 18 the
price of silver neared $18, and exchange officials were trying
to find out from the longs what their intentions were with
respect to the contracts. The Comex bullion dealers were
becoming increasingly uneasy at the inexorable rise in silver
they had helped to create. Probably things would have
worked out much better for the bullion dealer members of
the Comex board if the longs had let go, had they been
willing to sell their contracts rather than holding out for
delivery of physical metal.

Instead, the evidence grew that the longs did not intend
to let go, and that the shorts who had overhedged (sold more
contracts than they could meet from physical metal on hand
or expected deliveries) might be headed for bankruptcy.

The Comex board includes representatives of at least four
of the five or six largest bullion dealers. These are Dr. Henry
Jarecki, chairman of Mocatta Metals; Edward W. Hoffstatter
Jr., of Sharps, Pixley; Raymond Nessim of the Philipp Broth-
ers division of Engelhard Industries; and Herbert Coyne of
J. Aron & Co.

To suggest that these gentlemen are anything but busi-
nessman-honest would be doing them an injustice. But their
personal capital and that of their firms is continually at risk,
and since the dealings of these firms is conducted with all
the secrecy of the Soviet KGB, it is interesting to speculate
on their maneuvers to persuade the longs to let go during
a time when the Comex board was convinced that the silver
market was plunging toward a crisis.

The board met at least thirty-four times between September 1979 and the end of March 1980, a period when the
normal procedure would have called for monthly meetings,
seven in all, not thirty-four.

As a psychiatrist, Dr. Jarecki is presumably skilled in comprehending what motivates people, a factor, no doubt, in his success as an arbitrager. He became interested in silver trading after his brother Richard, also a physician, appeared at his home in New Haven, Conn., one day in the late 1960s bearing a shoe box full of one-dollar bills, each redeemable for silver at the Treasury. Drawn by the lure of silver, he built Mocatta Metals into one of the largest privately held corporations in America. His business success and his undoubted intellectual brillance made him a figure of power and influence during 1979, his first year on the Comex board.

The record indicates that while his suggestions were influential within the Comex board, he carefully avoided casting votes that would have involved him in a conflict of interest.

On September 4 Dr. Jarecki suggested raising the Comex margin for original new positions from $2,000 to $3,000. This is the minimum in cash that a hedger or speculator must deposit with his broker in order to control one 5,000-ounce contract on either the long or the short side. The board followed Dr. Jarecki's suggestion. On September 6 he suggested raising the margin to $5,000 and expanding daily trading limits. The board agreed. On September 12, 1979, Dr. Jarecki suggested that Comex should keep the CFTC closely informed on the silver situation—and especially on the growing December 1979 open interest. And so it went.

Perhaps as window dressing—and certainly as a gesture to please the regulators and the media—Comex created a special Silver Committee headed by Andrew Brimmer, a former Federal Reserve governor and one of the public members of the Comex board. Others on the Silver Committee included Oscar Burchard of Ore & Chemical Corporation, an old friend of Dr. Jarecki's, who had done plenty of options business with him; Henry Eisenberg, president of Brandeis Goldsmid; a base metals dealer John Morace, representing the floor brokers; Dave Johnston, head of commodities at

E. F. Hutton; and Mark Powers, head of commodities at Thomson McKinnon.

The committee's first meeting was attended by a quorum of members and was legally constituted. Other meetings were held in which members voted by telephone. These proceedings were of questionable legality under Comex bylaws. To the silver longs it was apparent that the Silver Committee had been created for one purpose: to persuade the longs at the Comex commission houses to liquidate their contracts.

Soon another influence began to be felt. Andrew Brimmer, as a former member of the Federal Reserve Board, had maintained close links with the Fed, and particularly with Paul Volcker, the Fed chairman. Through Brimmer the Comex was informed that the Fed was deeply concerned that the high price of silver would have an adverse effect on the dollar in the international markets. Most people who were aware of the message were convinced it came straight from the Federal Reserve chairman.

To a dispassionate onlooker this concern seemed a little puzzling. The government, as custodian of the world's largest gold supply (more than 260 million ounces at that time) and 139.5 million ounces of silver, saw the value of its hoard increase with every rise in the precious metals markets.

But the ways of the bureaucracy and its servants are complex and puzzling. Mr. Volcker has never been known as a hard money man; he sees gold and silver as alternatives and rivals to the dollar, and seeks to divorce the fortunes of the dollar from those of silver and gold. Mr. Volcker's commitment is to the integrity of the dollar, not to silver and gold, which since biblical times have been behind circulating money, including the paper currency with which America once conducted its cash transactions.

While Mr. Volcker may have had little reason to register concern at the rising prices for precious metals in the fall of 1979, Walter Goldschmidt, then president of Conti-Commodity Services, Inc., felt growing concern with the publicity given to the sayings and doings of Norton Waltuch, the world's second ranking silver bull, a vice president of Conti. Walter Goldschmidt, who is also executive vice president of Conti's parent company, the Continental Grain Company, knew that his boss, Michel Fribourg, the fifth generation descendant of the founder of the grain company, frowned upon excess publicity and certainly did not want any executive of his subsidiary to be accused of igniting a futures market or inciting it to go higher by simply appearing on the trading floor of the exchange.

Mr. Goldschmidt voluntarily appeared before the Comex board in September 1979 to assure the board that Conti and its customers would not precipitate a squeeze on the December delivery. Holders of a substantial portion of December futures would switch to March, May, or July 1980 deliveries, and would cooperate to insure the proper functioning of the silver markets. In early September, in fact, Mr. Goldschmidt directed all Conti branches in the U.S. and abroad to take no new positions in either the September or December silver Comex futures, and specified that positions already in such contracts would be for liquidation only.

Naturally, the New Jersey silver bull observed his boss's directive and did not add to his September or December long positions at Conti. But some of Norton's customers were unwilling to abide by Mister Goldschmidt's liquidation—only order and insisted on placing orders for silver futures with other Comex members who were more than willing to accept the business.

In this situation, the Comex Silver Committee began to investigate all Comex clearing members to try to ascertain information about customers' positions. Eventually, by mid-October, Comex's director of research, David Rutledge, reported that the large accounts at Conti held almost half the open interest in the Comex December delivery.*

---

*Mr. Rutledge is now an executive at the Sidney, Australia, commodity exchange and is thus beyond easy subpoena for any House or Senate committee wishing to delve more deeply into records that Comex might prefer to keep confidential.

The total open interest at that time in the Comex December delivery stood at 13,053 contracts, of which five bullion dealers were short 5,055 contracts, or something more than 25 million ounces of silver. Moreover, one of the trade houses—indeed the first to which Congress handed a virtual monopoly in 1978 to sell dealer options on gold, silver, platinum, and copper—had not only to supply daily variation margins for its Comex shorts; it had also to mark-to-the-market daily by sending money to the custodian banks segregating the premium monies for the benefit of the options holders. Thus Mocatta Metals had added daily exposure as the price of silver went up, an exposure from marking-to-the-market against favorable outstanding precious metals options, in addition to supplying Comex with variation margins.

To add a bit of spice to both the board meetings of Comex and the growing worries of Walter Goldschmidt and Conti executives, let alone Continental Grain executives, a summons was served on the Comex, Conti, Norton Waltuch, et al., by a disgruntled group of shorts who had entered the silver market on the wrong side during the second week in September 1979. These shorts had been wiped out with losses by covering on or before October 5. They accused the defendants of conspiring to manipulate the U.S. silver market. Their summons and complaint were dated October 15, 1979.

Early in the morning of October 18, 1979, the board of directors of the Chicago Board of Trade met in extraordinary session. It was rather bizarre for a number of reasons, including its length. While it continued, the opening of the market in silver futures was delayed for two hours and twenty minutes.

The meeting was also bizarre because Ralph Peters, chairman of the world's largest futures exchange, did not enter the conference room during the proceedings. Instead, he paced nervously in the corridor outside the meeting room door. His unusual absence from an important meeting of a board he chaired rested on a concept that, because he held extensive open positions in silver contracts, he had to disqualify himself to avoid any possible conflict of interest.

Such sterling abstinence, of course, did not cross the mind of Dr. Jarecki when months later, at his suggestion, Comex formed a special silver margin committee consisting of three members, which the good doctor chaired and which was primarily responsible for suggesting the rules that the Comex board adopted to break the silver market on January 21, 1980.

But back on October 18, 1979, as the directors of the CBOT straggled almost silently out of their meeting room, Paul Johns, executive vice president of the exchange, confided to a friend: "The question we are looking at is whether we are still looking at an orderly market."

Oddly enough, the Chicago board concluded that an orderly market still existed, even though the price of contracts had swung more in one day than in the fourteen years from 1951 to 1964.

At the Comex in New York on the same day the Silver Committee held a phone-quorum meeting, heard that the CBOT had taken into account the large positions held on that exchange by the Hunts, and had considered but rejected putting on a liquidation-only rule. This would have barred buyers and sellers from adding to their positions. But the Comex board heard from Fred DeFeo of the Comex Clearing Association that no clearing member was in trouble; and, like the Chicago board, decided not to adopt a liquidation-only rule.

In retrospect, the board's decision not to act on that date is understandable and possibly commendable. To be better oriented in regard to what happened to the price of silver after the third week of August, see Chart A. We will return later to an examination of the causes of silver's unprecedented rise.

Notice that after a sudden surge during the last few days

CHART A
SILVER BASE PRICE

Daily Cash

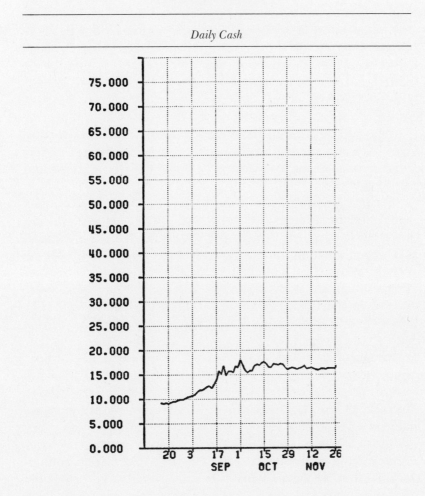

of August and through September, silver traded rather quietly and in a rather narrow range during October and November. There were a number of reasons for this apparent stability. For one thing, the bullion dealers expected the silver bulls to switch or liquidate their massive long positions; the idea of a massive demand for delivery of physical silver had not yet penetrated into the market's thinking. Second, the Silver Users Association was engaged in its lobbying campaign to persuade the government to dispose of part of its silver stockpile. The third reason for the brief period of price stability involved international politics. The U.S. had not yet decided to boycott the 1980 summer Olympics in Moscow, and U.S.-Soviet relations were in a relatively tranquil period. Further, the U.S. was still trying to negotiate in friendly fashion with the new revolutionary government of Iran; the hostage crisis had not yet erupted to generate new tensions and alarms.

Perhaps another logical reason for the silver price stability from the third week in September 1979 through the last week in November was simply widespread unawareness of the silver positions of the Hunts. They simply had not received the kind of publicity afforded billionaires in other fields. That was soon to change, and the media would lavish on the Hunts a kind of attention unparalleled since John D. Rockefeller gave away dimes during the great depression of the 1930s.

Meanwhile, in London ring-trading members of the London Metal Exchange (LME) became increasingly alarmed at the strains put on their normally orderly market by foreign buyers seeking both spot metal and three-month forward deliveries.

The LME does not trade American-style futures contracts. At LME the contracts involve delivery of an agreed amount of metal at an agreed price at an agreed date, called the "prompt date." Thus, if a silver bull went long one LME forward contract at 600 pence, he would be entitled to receive delivery of the metal precisely three months after the date of the trade, unless that date fell on a weekend or holiday. On the delivery date, the buyer would receive a warehouse receipt for the metal and make payment to the seller.

In the meantime, from the date of issuance of the contract the speculator or hedger owning the forward purchase could sell the metal (go short) for the same prompt date. Thus, at any time up to the prompt date the holder of a long contract or a short contract can liquidate his risk simply by making an opposite trade for the same amount of silver for the same prompt date. If a long holds a contract for June 30 silver at 600 pence and that silver is selling for 700 pence a few days before June 30, the liquidation of his contract generates a gain of 100 pence per ounce on the 10,000-ounce standard LME contract, or a profit of 10,000 pounds sterling before the round-turn commission.

Of course, if the long made his purchase at 700 pence and had to liquidate at 600 pence, his loss before commissions would be 10,000 sterling.

Silver has been traded in the LME ring since the nineteenth century in a free market atmosphere, where there are no daily price limits nor any position limits. The LME, with more than a hundred years of trading experience, holds that prices in the physical (cash) market lead forward prices. The ring members use no clearinghouse but rather confirm to each other.

London-style futures trading is almost like gambling in a casino. Each speculator or commercial client has a line of credit, the amount of exposure allotted by the trading member to the customer. All debits and credits are settled on the prompt dates on which they occur.

On the evening of October 18, 1979, at the Grosvenor House in London, the largest gathering of gentlemen in evening clothes in all history convened for the annual LME dinner. By no accident, the leading topic at almost every table happened to be silver. One of the leading brokerage-advisory firms in London had misread the silver market early in the year and had gone to the wall. The old-time ring member, to whom the adviser-broker owed more than a million pounds sterling, took over the business in lieu of collecting the debt. That is how Rudolf Wolff, a 114-year-old metal broker and dealer, found itself in the commodity advisory business.

Another topic of conversation among the black-tied gentlemen was the sudden reversal of roles played by the LME and the American metal exchanges. Traditionally, the action in London silver set the tone for the activity five or six hours later in New York and Chicago. But from the third week in August 1979 it had become painfully obvious to the London metals traders that New York and Chicago were in fact setting the tone for London trading the following day. In fact, it was to become apparent that from September 1979 through March 1980 the action on American exchanges would both lead and influence the physical silver markets around the world.

While the London brokers and dealers daily grew more concerned about the effect of American futures activity on world silver prices, the commissioners of the CFTC were becoming increasingly alarmed about possible manipulation in the silver pits.

What concerned the Comex board members was the prospect of a congestion in approaching delivery months. Congestion meant the existence of so many buy or long contracts in the hands of a few speculators that the shorts would be unable to deliver the metal and would have to deal with the longs from a position of weakness. To help relieve the pressure on the shorts, the CBOT ruled that, effective October 26, no trader could hold more than six hundred silver contracts. The rule was extended to provide that by February 1, 1980, speculators would have to reduce their positions to no more than six hundred contracts—3 million ounces—for any delivery month. In the industry the reaction to this rule could be summed up in three comments: the CBOT was "running scared"; the rule was too harsh; it would encourage traders to pull out of CBOT and take their business to Comex.

The Comex board secretly welcomed the action of the CBOT board, and the Comex chairman, Lowell Mintz, told the CFTC: "Comex must act in the best interests of all its market participants on the basis of its own independent and professional judgment."

To be kind to Mr. Mintz, who is no longer a participant in the silver pits, it is apparent that he spoke from expediency rather than from reality. And he will probably discover that lawyers who are interested in winning lawsuits depend upon the realities rather than expediencies.

And now it is time to delve into the actual situation in the silver market and to chronicle the events that caused billions of dollars to change hands in a very short period of time, and set up a field day for the lawyers of speculators who lost billions on both the rise and the fall of the silver price between the third week of August 1979 and the end of March 1980.

*

FIVE

*

THE
SILVER
SITUATION

While the Book of Genesis mentions gold much earlier than silver during the description of the Garden of Eden, it suggests that gold is wealth, silver is dignity. The use of silver to bury a loved one in biblical times may not have too much to do with the burial of many millions of dollars during the ascent and descent of the silver price in both cash and futures markets from the third week in August 1979 through the end of March 1980. A simple way to depict the price action for that period in the cash market appears in Chart B.

The first time I saw the following chart I envisioned climbing the Matterhorn and then falling off. If we follow the path of the silver price to its zenith of 50 on January 20, 1980, and then down to the depths of $10.80 an ounce on March 28, 1980, the magnitude of the swings becomes indelibly apparent. Tracing that path through its great moves

43

CHART B
SILVER BASE PRICE

Daily Cash

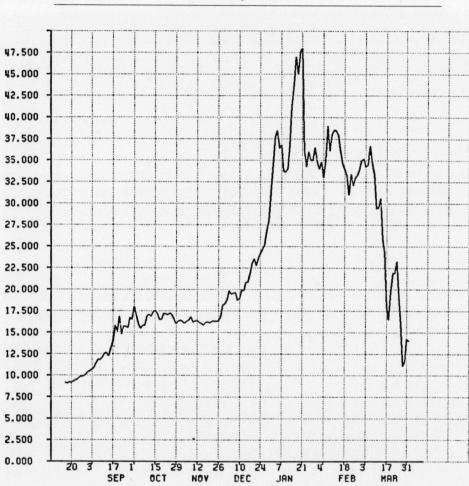

and severe reversal raises some significant questions: (1) Who had the most motivation to break the silver price? and (2) Who profited from the fall, and how?

To answer these questions it is best to start at the beginning of the price pattern shown above and try to reconstruct what actually happened.

The trigger that set off the initial silver price explosion from the third week in August to the first of October happened to be, oddly enough, the United States Government. Until August 21, 1979, the Treasury, which had conducted monthly gold auctions regularly since May 1978, customarily supplied gold from each auction to America's leading bullion dealers. The monthly gold auctions themselves were of course not handled by the Treasury Department, they were conducted by the General Services Administration (GSA).

The leading bullion dealers—Mocatta, Aron, Philipp Brothers, Sharps, Pixley, NMR, and others—customarily went short in the gold markets a few days before each auction, planning to buy gold at auction at a price lower than the level of the futures contracts. The arbitrage between the higher futures price and the lower auction price provided steady profits each month for the professional bullion dealers.

Sure enough, as the date of the August auction approached, the price of gold in both the physical and futures markets advanced while the bullion dealers went short. Naturally, they simultaneously entered bids at below the market price for the Midas metal from the government stocks. Indeed, Patrick Henry once admitted: "I have but one lamp by which my feet are guided, and that is the lamp of experience." And the experience of America's bullion dealers at each monthly GSA auction proved profitable because they were awarded generally most of the gold they had bid for.

But in the auction of August 21 the GSA saw fit to award 720,000 ounces of the 750,000 ounces offered to the Dresdner Bank of West Germany. The balance of 30,000 ounces went to other foreign banks. The U.S. bullion dealers did not get a single ounce of the Treasury's gold.

Mocatta and the other large bullion dealers are heavily financed by friendly banks, and they cannot suffer prolonged market exposure. So the following morning, as if they were one person, the disappointed dealers went into the London market to cover their shorts.

The bullion dealers were fully aware that for almost a century the price of silver has worked together with the price of gold so that the buying action to cover the unsatisfied gold shorts would almost certainly raise the price of gold at the London fixing. If that occurred, silver would become more valuable. The bullion dealers, therefore, acted on the almost certain premise that if gold went up, so would silver. Thus, when they bought gold that morning to cover their exposure on the aborted short sales, the dealers went long silver in the London market. What they lost on the gold trade was to be buffered by the profits in silver.

The sudden surge in the gold price, accompanied by simultaneous demand in the silver market, triggered an explosion that found its way into American silver pits that same morning in New York and Chicago. The stage was set for the first killing by the silver bulls.

A commission house is a firm that acts as agent for customers and earns its profits basically from commissions generated on customers' orders and interest earned on customers' funds held in the firm's accounts. The goal of every good account executive slaving for the enrichment of his commission house is (a) to raise continual risk capital for trading purposes; and (b) to increase the equity of that capital.

Norton Waltuch realized that his light had long been hidden under a bushel (except for occasional mention in financial columns) and that publicity would help him raise equity capital. In order to increase the equity capital that would flow into his accounts he had to risk the funds in futures contracts. Since his firm offered only brokerage service in commodity futures trading, and a subsidiary of his firm offered investment in shares of manage money funds and pools, part of which came under his advice and direction, his behavior from the time he began to get publicity in August 1979 in the *Wall Street Journal* becomes understandable.

Assuredly, on the morning in August that the bullion dealers in America were skunked out of the gold auction by the GSA Norton knew all about it as he hurried to his Jaguar parked in his driveway.

And just as assuredly he began a concentrated campaign to implement his trading plan.

Every futures trader with imagination and talent goes into a specific commodity armed with a trading plan. Simply put, the trading plan involves the following factors:

1. Preset entry points—a price level at which the trader will enter the market.
2. Preset exit points, where the trader will realize profits.
3. Stop-loss points, where the trader will absorb his losses and limit his exposure in adverse markets.

The astute trader will have a plan for the useful employment of monies and equity generated if the market is favorable and a plan for averaging prices down by adding contracts if the market retreats temporarily. He will have a sensible cash reserve to supply variation margins if the market is temporarily adverse.

Most of all, every seasoned futures trader dreams of getting in on the beginning of a major move in the price of a listed commodity, holding some positions to take advantage of the price trend, meanwhile going in and out of the market with some positions, using the ensuing profits to cushion any possible future losses if the trend temporarily reverses.

Rest assured that Norton Waltuch carefully structured and monitored his silver trading plan for himself and his customers. Since the only way he could generate profits for himself and his clients was through profitable futures trading, he had to *manage* the monies committed at risk—and he felt he had a sure thing in silver as long as the markets remained neutral.

By "neutral" it is inferred that the normal forces of price change on futures or any other exchanges that rely on supply and demand of orders would prevail on the trading floor—without bias on the part of the rule-makers serving on the board of directors of the involved exchange for any particular segment of the membership.

But as events from the third week of August 1979 until the end of March 1980 clearly indicate, neither the Chicago Board of Trade nor the New York Commodity Exchange was allowed to function as a neutral market.

Of course, Norton Waltuch and the other silver bulls could hardly have anticipated the Comex board's bias for the silver shorts. This bias was to destroy the market's neutrality, which had previously prevailed under the exchange rules, providing more or less fair opportunity for traders going long or short in the futures market.

Now Norton knows the silver futures markets about as well as any living trader, having been at risk in its treacheries ever since silver futures made their debut on Comex and CBOT. The silver markets have always been big and liquid, and have attracted a large following of speculators. This has benefited hedgers, those who have to shift the risks of future price changes. At least one expert who has written prolifically on taming the pits believed that before August 1979 the silver markets were murder to most traders trying to trade the trend. The markets have killed traders with whipsaw losses, and been miserly with the big moves that herald handsome profits. But when the market killed, it tended to kill with a fine impartiality, not because the exchange's board of directors willed it so.

There were few exceptions to this rule of neutrality, that is, until the fall of 1979.

In 1978 Comex rules set $1,000 as minimum margin—the amount a customer had to deposit in cash with his broker— to position a long or short silver contract. The daily limit move up or down from the previous day's settlement was twenty cents an ounce, or $1,000 on a 5,000-ounce contract. Thus, while long-term trends in the silver market appeared infrequently, it was not difficult for a trader to make or lose 100 percent of his margin within a single week.

That is why that until the fall of 1979 the silver pits were filled with short-term traders who tried to make money from silver price changes, either by going short on strength and covering on weakness, or buying on weakness and selling on strength. The position traders simply put on the longs or the shorts, as they envisioned the market, and accumulated their positions so that they had a mathematical price advantage.

Norton Waltuch, of course, knew intimately the situation inside the silver pits of New York and Chicago. He had studied the fundamentals affecting the supply and demand of the physical metal, and, being well informed, naturally realized that the supply of newly mined silver around the world was insufficient to meet the growing demand from third world countries, China, the USSR and the United States. The outlook was for a dwindling world supply of silver.

After long deliberation and study, he concluded that the proper manner to make profits from silver futures was to trade from the long side (buy on weakness and sell on strength), while adding to existing long positions as the price of silver rose and the accounts generated increased equity.

Table I shows the prices, net change, and open interest in the December '79 and March '80 Comex silver contracts during the latter part of August 1979.

On August 21 the settlement price for the December 5,000-ounce contract on Comex stood at $9.59 per ounce. A total of 23,783 contracts was outstanding, representing 118,915,000 ounces of silver. The March '80 contract that same day traded at $9.80, and the open interest—the sum

Table I
Settlement Price/Prev. Day Open Interest:
Comex Silver—August 1979

Trade Date	Dec. '79 Silver Price	Daily Net Change	Prev. Day Open Int.	Mar. '80 Silver Price	Daily Net Change	Prev. Day Open Int.
21	9.59	+20	22,844	9.80	+20	28,716
22	9.78	+19	23,783	9.993	+19.3	28,498
23	9.98	+20	23,841	10.193	+20	28,444
24	10.165	+18.5	24,812	10.393	+20	28,641
27	10.190	+2.5	25,246	10.432	+3.9	28,739
28	10.39	+20	25,918	10.632	+20	28,703
29	10.535	+14.5	26,692	10.77	+13.8	29,370
30	10.735	+20	27,495	10.97	+20	29,568
31	10.86	+12.5	28,096	11.045	+7.5	29,744

of the long contracts and the short contracts divided by two—stood at 28,716, or 143,580,000 ounces.

To anyone working out the arithmetic it might have seemed unusual that the silver involved in just those two deliveries was more than five times the amount actually available in grade to fulfill the delivery requirements of the exchange. But as a matter of fact, the open interest in both December and March was *less* than for some contracts in 1978, a rather quiet year, if we compare the price action to 1977 rather than to 1979.

Open interest is actually very important to traders using the technical approach. The theory is:

1. If the price is rising and the open interest is rising, there will be momentum for a further rise.

2. If the open interest is falling while the price is rising, a reversal is near at hand and the price could quickly change direction and fall.

3. If the price is falling and the open interest is rising, then momentum is building to pressure the continuance of the decline.

4. If the open interest is declining while the price is falling, a reversal is near at hand and the price could quickly change direction and rise.

Immediately after the misdirected GSA auction of August 21 the spot (cash) month on which there was no daily trading limit was August. On August 21 the settlement price for this delivery stood at $9.37. The open interest had leaped from a mere sixteen contracts on August 20 to 341 on August 21. So somebody had to know something was going to happen in Washington. It will be of interest to find out some day who were the buyers, because on August 22 the open interest dropped to eighty-six, and the holders of 255 contracts for 1,275,000 ounces had to gross over a quarter of a million dollars overnight on a price move of 20 cents an ounce.

But in the other months the price action appeared normal

and the market neutral. The September delivery, which would become the spot month on August 29, indicated a normally declining pattern in the open interest. There was no indication of an impending squeeze on the September shorts or a possible corner in the September, December, or March Comex silver contracts.

Oddly enough, during the last week in August the media, led by the *Wall Street Journal,* began to air intimations of possible hanky-panky in the silver pits. Some of the spotlight began to shine on both Norton Waltuch and his company, ContiCommodity Services Inc., a wholly owned subsidiary of the Continental Grain Company.

Norton Waltuch, who had managed the New York office for Conti since 1970, had moved up in 1978 into Conti-Capital, to devote full time to managing other people's money. He also gave close attention to his own funds, and to those of close friends and business associates. Sharing ContiCapital's management responsibility at that time were Ivan Auer, Conti senior vice president, formerly in charge of all research, and Tom Waldeck, a Geneva-based expert for the Continental Grain Company. Since the managers of these monies were to receive a fee based on profitability, Waltuch and his associates had a special incentive to win.

Waltuch enjoyed the publicity that followed when he appeared on the Comex floor wearing the bright yellow Conti trading jacket (size 48) and waving his arms briskly as he strode purposefully toward the roaring pits. A commanding figure of a man, well over six feet tall, Waltuch has always believed that the great private fortunes of the world were made from private information. As August ended, Waltuch knew and fervently believed that going long silver and staying long had to be a concept whose time had come.

An old saw in the commodities trade says that an optimist believes the market is going up and a pessimist is a person who believes the optimist may be right.

As August 1979 moved into its final days, another of the market's major figures became increasingly nervous about the course of the price of silver. Henry Jarecki, chairman of Mocatta Metals, over six feet tall, handsome, urbane, debonair, also reads the *Wall Street Journal* along with other publications each morning, and he realized that the publicity involving Norton Waltuch could help to generate a malignantly growing bullishness in the marketplace. Dr. Jarecki and his brother Richard like to leave nothing to chance. They and their firms (Mocatta, Brody White) are constantly at risk in volatile markets, and Mocatta's exposure is assessed every day, if not every hour.

Mocatta is undoubtedly the largest grantor of precious metals options in America, because permission to market options in gold, silver, and platinum was granted to the firm by Congress in the act reauthorizing the CFTC in 1978.

Under the firm's agreement with the CFTC and with such commission merchants as Bache, Shearson, Conti, Merrill Lynch, etc., who vend Mocatta options to the retail public, Mocatta does not initially receive the option premiums received at the time of sale. But if the market rises, it must mark-to-the-market, that is, deposit cash to insure performance of its contracts, or deposit warehouse receipts to cover the metal involved, if the options are calls. Unlike a futures contract, a call option limits the risk of the holder to the premium paid for the call. At the end of August 1978, the position of Mocatta options was predominantly at a growing risk on the wrong side of the market, since it granted mostly precious metals calls. The affairs of Mocatta being quite secret, it is not possible for anyone outside the organization to know how many of the outstanding precious metals calls were hit naked (issued without the protection of either long physical silver or long futures). But it is known that Mocatta has never been fully hedged against its issued and outstanding calls. Mocatta has always made the bulk of its money from arbitrage and trading—and the monies generated in normal markets from earned premiums or existing premiums yet to be earned represent quite a cushion in the trading maneuvers of that aggressive bullion company.

Jarecki therefore realized that, in addition to the normal variation margin any bullion dealer has to deposit during rising markets to cover short positions, his firm would have to supply either warehouse receipts or mark-to-the-market money to custodian banks representing holders of Mocatta options. And so Jarecki decided he had to do something to solve the problems that would arise in the future if the price of silver kept appreciating in both the cash and futures markets.

The obvious ploy was to try and stop the buying activities of Norton Waltuch and his company in the marketplace so that the growing legend of an unlimited pocket book fueled by Middle Eastern oil money would not inflame the speculative lust and greed of the uninformed public, who had begun to smart under the whip of growing gas and food prices and ever increased taxation.

One way to break the power of the legend was to spread stories that the longs were attempting a squeeze on the September contracts. These tales might bring back memories of the squeeze that failed in January 1974. Then the Hunts had had at least one large short in the bag; Mocatta had been short more than 35 million ounces of silver while the price of silver had skyrocketed, from $3.33 an ounce for spot metal at the end of 1973 to well over $6 an ounce for the February 1974 delivery. Speculators had rushed into long positions, believing that Mocatta would be unable to make delivery to the Hunts, who were the major buyers. But deliveries had been effected with the help of the Bank of Mexico, sending the price of silver into a plunge.

Could the buying surge at the end of August and the beginning of September 1979 signal another squeeze on the shorts? The newspapers seemed to think so, and the bullion dealers, who were well represented on the Comex board, and who would have to supply the short side of the silver market in event of a public buying spree, geared themselves for the coming onslaught with the silver bulls.

One of the ways to discourage excessive public speculation

in commodity futures contracts in any market is to increase the margin a speculator must deposit to buy more contracts. If this higher margin is made retroactive to existing positions, some of the longs will obviously let go, easing the pressure on the shorts. So on September 4, 1979, at a Comex board meeting, Dr. Jarecki suggested that silver margins be raised to $3,000 a contract, and daily trading limits doubled from twenty to forty cents. The board so ruled.

Two days later, when the September contract had moved from $11.02 to $11.80 an ounce, the doctor again suggested to the board that margins should be raised to $5,000 and that variable trading limits be adopted. The board agreed.

It was also revealed at this meeting that of the 29,944 December open interest there were eighteen longs with more than two hundred contracts each, including nine accounts holding a thousand or more contracts. These large holders represented 79 percent of the long side of the open interest.

Of the twenty-four shorts holding more than two hundred contracts each, ten were short more than a thousand contracts each. These ten shorts represented 73 percent of the short side of the open interest.

By this time in early September press reports had established that Conti was playing a leading role on the long side of the market. The attention of the shorts focused on Norton Waltuch and how to stop him.

The annual dinner of the Comex is normally held at the Waldorf-Astoria in the second week of September. In 1979 this black-tie affair was held on September 11. That evening a large turnout of tuxedoed members, friends, female guests, and employees of the exchange and its member firms filled the grand ballroom of the Waldorf to its balconies. The Meyer Davis Society Orchestra played schmaltzy music, even though that afternoon silver had closed on an ominously steady upnote. December delivery silver stood at $12.89 after a rise of $1.63 an ounce since the first trading day of the month, just one week earlier.

At Conti's table were Mr. and Mrs. Goldschmidt, Mr. and

Mrs. Waltuch, the author and his wife, Harry Marshall, Conti's New York chief of operations, and a friend, and Mr. and Mrs. Dave Albertson, close friends of the Waltuchs. That table was one of the few in the room where the faces were happy. All happiness seemed to have vanished from the surrounding tables, occupied by bullion dealers like Mocatta, who happened to be short.

Toward the end of the evening Dr. Jarecki passed by the Conti table and signaled me to come over and chat with him. I excused myself and joined Henry in a corner of the corridor outside the ballroom.

He came right to the point: "I'd like to ask you some questions."

Instinctively I knew he was going to ask about the silver market, and my instant reaction was to give him the military response I had learned as a U.S. Army officer: name, rank, and serial number. But he was visibly agitated, and since we have been quite friendly for over a decade, I could see little harm in volunteering, "Go right ahead and ask."

His very first question was "How much buying power does Norton have?"

For a moment I chewed on this request for a breach of confidence, then smilingly shot back, "Henry, how the hell do I know how much buying power Norton has? I'm Conti's New York research director, not its operations director."

With a sigh he asked next, "How do we stop this?" His phrasing suggested that Norton was doing something improper, something detrimental to the industry.

I suggested, "Why don't you ask your brother Richard?"

Dr. Richard Jarecki is a computer genius, who once devised a program that broke the casino in San Remo. As a younger man the doctor had stood before a roulette wheel, a terminal in his pocket linked to an off-casino computer that told him after input from the wheel's spins what numbers to bet. Richard Jarecki is also the genius who, as we have related, years earlier appeared at his brother Henry's home in New Haven with the batch of silver dollars that launched the brothers on their successful careers in the silver market. For the past few years Richard has enjoyed trading on the Comex floor.

But Henry Jarecki shrugged off my well-intentioned suggestion and prodded me further with "Come on. How would you do it?"

So I simply said, "Whenever any large orders to buy show up in the pits several minutes before closing time, I would offer 5,000 to 10,000 contracts at the market. . . ."

At this he wrinkled his nose, rolled his eyes heavenward, patted me on the back (Henry is about 6′3″ while I am barely 5′9″), and walked away mumbling "Thank you."

Since there would obviously be no squeeze on the September delivery because of the small open interest, the attention of the Comex board shifted to the December delivery. Some of the board members spoke openly about possible manipulation and possible market "congestion" (a situation in which most of the open interest on one side is held in very few hands).

Actually, the day after the Comex dinner Henry Jarecki proposed to his fellow Comex board members that Comex and the CFTC should maintain close communication with regard to the situation in December silver.

At this point Walter Goldschmidt, then president of Conti, voluntarily appeared before the Comex to assure those worthies that there would be no squeeze and that December positions would be rolled over or reduced well in advance of the delivery month.

Walter Goldschmidt, now in his early fifties, with silver hair and a professorial bearing, has worked for the Continental Grain Company since he turned eighteen. He is a soft-spoken, dignified man, who has kept a low profile, avoided media attention, and yet within the industry is well known, respected by his peers and by the more than 18,000 employees worldwide over whom he holds management control as executive vice president of the grain company. His word is good, and when he told the directors of the Comex that no squeeze was intended or would be effected, few doubted that he acted in good faith, or that his forecast of the silver situation would be correct.

Adding to his verbal assurances, he sent a letter to Comex asserting that Conti's customers would switch a substantial portion of their December positions to March, May, or July 1980 deliveries, and that Conti would cooperate to insure continuance of a properly functioning futures market.

And in what condition was the Comex silver market in mid-September? Table II indicates the condition of the December and March deliveries for that autumn month:

It is immediately obvious to any observer familiar with Comex statistics that if the shorts were fully hedged—if they held an ounce of silver in safekeeping for every ounce they were short—they would not be in peril. This would be true even if the longs decided to acquire all the silver they had contracted to buy.

It was also plain to industry watchers familiar with Conti and Mr. Goldschmidt that when he issued an order by telex in early September forbidding all offices from acquiring new long positions for any customer for September or December, that order would be obeyed.

Naturally, Norton Waltuch is a Comex member and could buy September and December contracts through other clearing members. Rumors that he might do this evidently reached some Comex directors. On September 17 the Comex board expressed concern about the accuracy of Conti's statement that it would not add to long positions for September or December. With this, the board passed a resolution declaring the existence of market congestion (their opinion, of course) and asking Conti to present within twenty-four hours a plan for resolving the situation.

Within the deadline, Conti stated its willingness (1) to reduce December longs at the firm by one-third (from 6,000 contracts to 4,000 contracts) by September 26, and (2) to reduce the customers' long positions to a maximum of 2,000

TABLE II
SETTLEMENT PRICE/PREV. DAY OPEN INTEREST:
COMEX SILVER—SEPT. 1979

Trade Date	Dec. '79 Silver Price	Daily Net Change	Prev. Day Open Int.	Mar. '80 Silver Price	Daily Net Change	Prev. Day Open Int.
4	11.26	+40	29,552	11.445	+40	29,841
5	11.66	+40	29,944	11.845	+40	29,636
6	12.06	+40	28,446	12.245	+40	29,804
7	12.19	+13	29,089	12.34	+9.5	30,203
10	12.59	+40	27,752	12.74	+40	30,634
11	12.89	+30	26,903	13.044	+30.4	30,898
12	12.50	−39	26,918	12.665	−37.9	31,464
13	12.90	+40	26,891	13.065	+40	31,590
14	13.30	+40	27,641	13.465	+40	32,458
17	13.90	+60	26,262	14.065	+60	32,997
18	14.70	+80	24,669	14.865	+80	33,068
19	15.50	+80	25,622	15.665	+80	33,196
20	15.70	+20	22,339	15.89	+22.5	32,838
21	16.10	+40	20,596	16.29	+40	33,519
24	16.38	+28	19,631	16.68	+39	33,016
25	15.78	−60	19,442	16.08	−60	33,099
26	16.10	+32	19,440	16.47	+39	32,720
27	16.50	+40	20,325	16.87	+40	32,423
28	16.80	+30	19,946	17.19	+32	32,422

December contracts no later than one week prior to the first notice day for the December contract (November 23, 1979).

The first notice day is the first day that a short in a contract can tender the involved silver to the account of the long by issuing a tender notice (or "notice"). The long who is tendered a notice is considered "stopped" or is called a "stopper." He can then either accept delivery of the silver by handing the issuing clearing member (broker) a check for the physical silver, or he may "retender" the notice within twenty-four hours if he does not desire the metal. Thus the clearing broker can retender the notice to some other open long at a different firm at the market price the next day.

Conti, on September 19, also assured Comex that it would take other steps to reduce the pressure or "congestion" on the December contract. Customers would not be allowed to increase their long positions in December silver, and, further, the reductions would be accomplished by switches, EFP's, and other legal means of accomplishing the objective.

In retrospect, Conti's willingness to comply with the board's requests seems a little puzzling. But it must be remembered that Norton Waltuch always traded with a plan, and with an exit number in mind. In the case of December silver that exit price was probably in the area of $15 an ounce. On September 18 December silver stood at $14.70 an ounce, and appeared ready to move higher.

Meanwhile, in September, the December delivery was behaving in a gentlemanly, if bullish, fashion, following the pattern of other futures months. The futures had undergone eight days of limit-up trading and three days of lower-than-limit moves. On one bizarre day, September 12, the price dipped to $12.50.

It was in mid-September that the first stirrings of substantial silver purchases from Swiss banks on behalf of the USSR hit the London market, and on September 20 the price leaped 76 pence (about $1.60) in the LME ring. (Unlike trading on United States commodity exchanges, trading on the

London Metal Exchange since 1877 occurs in five-minute morning and afternoon "rings." These are brief sessions held by ring-members around a trading ring on the exchange floor that boasts a solitary ashtray in the center of the ring. But the prices made there affect metal prices all over the world.) The activity in the physicals spurred the demands of the Comex longs, and they had to be accommodated by the shorts. But now that daily trading limits on Comex had been expanded to 80 cents, small shorts were rapidly being wiped out, cleaned out and destroyed, concentrating the short side of the silver market into the tender ministrations of its bullion-dealing members.

The sudden spurt in silver prices abroad lifted values on the American exchanges and touched off new fears among the bullion dealers that even the higher trading limits would not control the runaway bulls. These fears were well warranted. As September melted into October, the spotlight moved away from the silver bull who lived in New Jersey to focus on the larger ones who lived in Dallas, Texas.

Since 1974 the Hunts had maintained sizable silver futures positions in both Chicago and New York, and for five years they had rolled over these futures into more distant months as the spot month neared or arrived. They never indicated any intention to accept delivery of the physical metal, since they could carry 5,000 ounces with only the $1,000 initial margin and whatever variation margins were required during declining silver markets. Moreover, the leverage cost them nothing like bank interest on the full value of physical metal.

But because of the innuendos aired in the financial press during September, and because the Hunts also maintained a very substantial open interest on Comex, rumors began to reach the ears of the CBOT directors that Hunt would not roll over his positions there when the spot months arrived.

This caused both alarm and action at the CBOT in October. Primary responsibility for monitoring the silver market at CBOT rests with twenty-seven professionals on the CBOT staff who work for the Office of Investigations and Audits (OIA) of the exchange. This office is an independent staff unit employing accountants, auditors, and investigators, who investigate and monitor the financial health of member firms, seek to uncover any rule violations, and play watchman in the various contracts traded on the exchange floor.

Contrast this professional investigative staff agency with the emergency Silver Committee of "disinterested parties" established on Comex and chaired by a former member of the Federal Reserve Board.

Despite the stable behavior of the silver price during October, the CBOT evidently felt that remedial action of a really radical nature was needed. The board concluded that an unprecedented number of contracts was being used to buy bullion rather than being canceled through liquidation in the futures pit. The directors evidently also felt that more and more speculators, seeking to acquire bullion through acceptance of delivery on long futures contracts, would enter the futures market, changing its character from a market of paper contracts.

Table III shows the daily price action and open interest levels of the December and the March deliveries on Comex during October:

Several observations are immediately evident:

1. Nothing spectacular happened to the contract prices in New York during October.
2. The open interest in both months rumored to be future targets for a squeeze or corner continued to decline. In New York on October 1 the December delivery stood at $17.20 per ounce; and on October 31, the last trading day of the month, the December contract settled at $16.79, or a net loss to position longs of forty-one cents an ounce for the month.

In Chicago, during October the silver price pattern seems

TABLE III

SETTLEMENT PRICE/PREV. DAY OPEN INTEREST: COMEX SILVER—OCT. 1979

Trade Date	Dec. '79 Silver Price	Daily Net Change	Prev. Day Open Int.	Mar. '80 Silver Price	Daily Net Change	Prev. Day Open Int.
1	17.20	+40	19,557	17.59	+40	32,325
2	17.30	+10	19,439	17.70	+11	32,181
3	17.31	+1	19,373	17.71	+1	32,345
4	16.91	−40	18,494	17.31	−40	33,561
5	16.51	−40	18,341	16.91	−40	33,118
8	15.91	−60	17,162	16.31	−60	32,001
9	16.71	+80	16,980	17.11	+80	31,852
10	17.51	+80	16,378	17.91	+80	31,449
11	17.80	+29	15,489	18.21	+30	30,757
12	17.80	0	15,220	18.23	+2	30,641
15	17.82	+2	15,138	18.30	+7	30,482
16	17.42	−40	14,870	17.90	−40	30,039
17	17.30	−12	13,779	17.85	−5	30,582
18	17.40	+10	13,617	18.05	+20	30,624
19	17.78	+38	13,053	18.33	+28	29,775
22	17.66	−12	12,951	18.21	−12	29,912
23	17.55	−11	13,031	18.16	−5	29,469
24	17.71	+16	13,156	18.33	+17	29,600
25	17.45	−26	12,763	18.06	−27	29,706
26	17.05	−40	12,756	17.66	−40	29,317
29	16.65	−40	12,454	17.26	−40	29,388
30	16.60	−5	12,183	17.17	−9	29,314
31	16.79	+19	11,994	17.36	+19	29,126

similar. On October 1 the spot month stood at $17.90, and by the last trading day the figure declined to $16.42, for a net drop in value of $1.48. The total CBOT open interest for all futures months in silver declined during October by more than 51,000 contracts.

On the morning of October 25, however, the CBOT board of directors invoked its temporary emergency powers and adopted a rule setting a limit of six hundred contracts per account for silver futures. Before this rule was enacted, speculators always had the right to go long or go short as many silver contracts as they desired or could afford. And assuredly the Hunts and their friends and family who had maintained roll-over positions in silver futures on the Comex and CBOT since 1974 had more than six hundred contracts each at the time CBOT adopted its restrictive rule.

It became perfectly apparent to those in the industry that the CBOT rule would affect the Hunts the most and that they would be compelled to shift their business elsewhere. Elsewhere meant either the Comex or the LME. Oddly enough, the Comex during October did not seriously consider establishing position limits to *squeeze* the longs. Instead, the Silver Committee, chaired by Dr. Brimmer, continued to "investigate" and "monitor" the activities of Conti accounts. And now the committee also turned its myopic orbs on the Hunts. The rationale for such surveillance stemmed from the complaint of the trade shorts (bullion firms) that longs in the hands of a few people, backed by sufficient cash reserves, could threaten the fair and orderly existence of silver futures trading.

Interestingly enough, the sentiment of the Comex and CBOT boards inclined toward making whatever rules were necessary to cause the longs to let go and to prevent a squeeze on the shorts. And, understandably, Dr. Jarecki, who is probably the world's leading authority on silver squeezes, prophesied ten months earlier the situation alleged to be building on both exchanges.

In an article published in *Euromoney,* March 1979, he outlined three ways to squeeze the silver market: (1) outright purchase, (2) sell switches, and (3) combination.

In the first instance the speculator buys 50 to 100 million ounces, causing the price to rise several dollars, just as it did when the Hunts purchased heavily in February 1974. The problem, then, is that if the speculator wants to sell, he will cause the price to collapse much faster than it rose. Jarecki, who evidently has the ability to see down the road at least a year or so ahead—especially if he has an important role in preparing the map—felt that the first method of outright purchase of silver bullion would fail primarily because of the cost of financing and storage. He also felt that the method of attempting to squeeze the silver market by selling switches (buying the spot month and simultaneously selling the forward month) could not succeed because of the high cost required to derive small benefits.

But his third method of initiating a silver squeeze could most likely be used, he said, if the manipulators bought 175 million ounces of nearby silver and sold only 150 million ounces forward through switches. Then, as the spreads between the two months narrowed and a shortage of physical silver emerged, the specter of looming silver shortages would cause public speculators to enter the market and cause the unhedged 25 million silver ounces to increase in value. He did admit that this route took the greatest amount of skill and the involvement of experienced market professionals.

What the good doctor failed to point out is that when there are *all buyers* in the silver pits, the shorts can be only the bullion dealers and not speculators who are going short unhedged.

In markets under buying stress, such as existed during the last week in August, small shorts who went along as the market rose were quickly wiped out. How did the markets rise? Not because of the continuing buying pressure from the longs but rather because the bullion dealer has to go short at a price higher than he paid for the silver bullion in order to be hedged.

Thus, an almost ironclad conclusion may be made about the price movements of any precious metal. It is this: When the price suddenly explodes, the major portion of the short side of the market is being made by the bullion dealers; they are marking up the price of the futures contract over and above the cost of buying and carrying the physicals that protect the short sales.

So what happened when, after a period of brief price explosion on the upside in September, silver went into a narrow trading channel in October?

The not so obvious answer is that the short side was being dominantly supplied by commercial firms who had to market silver as a production pattern, and simultaneously went short to insure themselves against a price drop.

Along with the bullion dealers, who normally hedge at whatever level they find the market to be, who else was selling? There were the producing mines, who have to sell silver every day. There could also have been some die-hard silver bears who *knew* commercial hedging was going on during October and expected a setback, in accordance with the law of futures gravity. That law simply is that whenever a price of a futures contract moves more than 50 percent in six months, the price is likely to experience a severe setback before resuming its rise. This is true if the underlying commodity is actually in a genuine rising price trend.

Helping along this concept of contrary opinion were several advisory services, who claimed that although silver had moved in ten months to a level about 300 percent above the price at the start of the year, the price had shot up too far and too fast for fundamental sensibility and that it could encounter a sudden setback to more respectable levels.

In retrospect, one may look with some compassion upon Alfredo Fonseca, the hedge-meister of Minero Peru Commercial (MINPECO), who overhedged severely during the month of October 1979.

His task was to protect his firm, an agency of the Peruvian

government that buys silver concentrate from Peruvian mines, has it refined in Mexico, and markets the refined silver some six months after the ore is mined. The agency's risk, of course, is that it may buy concentrate at a high price and, after a market decline, sell silver at a lower price. To assure a cash flow to MINPECO through the sale of metal and to hedge against market losses on silver it has bought in the form of concentrate, Fonseca's responsibility was to sell forward in London and at brokerage houses in New York just enough silver for future delivery to cover the metal MINPECO expected to receive each month of the year.

Fonseca, at twenty-five, had risen to a high post in the agency by being a smart, friendly fellow, ambitious and politically accepted in the revolutionary Peruvian regime. A lover of the niceties, including good food, he stood about 5'5" and weighed close to two hundred pounds.

For advice in his hedging operation he relied heavily on the giant commission houses in New York and London where his agency conducted its business. And in October 1979 there were very few, if any, silver bulls among the top brokerage houses, with the exception, of course, of ContiCommodity Services, ACLI International, and Rudolf Wolff in London.

In fact, the largest brokerage firm in the world, which was once bullish on America, but after observing the ineptitude of the American Administration changed its slogan to a breed apart, came right out and recommended silver as a sale rather than as a buy.

Perhaps because of the growing silver bearishness of most commission houses and investment advisory services during October, Fonseca decided that month to overhedge by going short 10 million more ounces for December delivery than the agency could possibly deliver.

This sale had a dampening influence on the silver market. So did publicity about the nearly certain enactment of a bill to resume sales from the U.S. government's silver stockpile of 139.5 million ounces. The presence of hedgers like MINPECO in the market forced bullion dealers like Mocatta,

J. Aron, and others to go excessively into the market, buy bullion, mark up their costs, and offer futures at a much higher price.

In effect, then, the bullion dealer, almost like the New York Stock Exchange specialist, causes the futures market in gold, silver, or platinum to rise only when the commercial firms and speculators of contrary opinion are absent from the market.

Since the silver markets in New York and Chicago remained relatively stable in October, and even declined a bit, it may be safely assumed that the bulk of the short selling at that time did not come from the bullion dealers.

And who was buying in October?

According to the press there were now at least two large buying influences in the silver markets: Group A, meaning the Hunts, their families, and allied corporations; and Group B, the "foreign investors," meaning Norton Waltuch, and Naji Nahas, the forty-five investors who did their buying through the Volksbank in Geneva,* and members of the Saudi Arabian silver connection, who evidently managed to maintain silver accounts at several large brokerage houses, including Conti. The Saudis were also quite close to the Hunts.

Rarely has a market been so carefully scrutinized as the silver market in October 1979. The directors of both Comex and CBOT had started making loud noises about possible market manipulation by the longs. The CFTC monitored the entire silver situation to assure itself that there was no collaboration or collusion between the market forces led by Norton Waltuch and his accounts; Naji Nahas, the Lebanese silver bull from Sao Paolo, Brazil; and Mahmoud Fustok, representing the friends and relatives of the reigning mon-

---

*The U.S. press usually refers to this institution as Banque Populaire, its new name, although money people in Geneva and Zurich tend to use its old name, Volksbank.

archy in Saudi Arabia. Obviously, if all these buyers, along with the forty-five foreign investors at the Banque Populaire, acted together, and in turn acted in concert with the Hunts, then the longs could dominate the shorts. In that case the concern of the exchanges and the CFTC might have been legitimate.

But the entire campaign by the exchanges to force the longs to let go of their December '79 and March '80 holdings in the fall of 1979 smelled like dead fish in the summer sun.

Further indications of interest arose in October from the Federal Reserve Board. Exchange officials were informed that the Federal Reserve was concerned because the rising price of silver and the soaring price of gold had a weakening effect on the dollar. Hogwash. The dollar kept losing its purchasing power because of inexorable inflation. Indeed, in October and November of 1979 the inflation snowball was rolling down the mountain. Before it was checked, Americans would drain millions of dollars from savings banks and mutual funds to try to get on the gold and silver train before the chance was gone.

In October Norton Waltuch, under pressure from his superiors to reduce the holdings in his accounts, was not doing much buying. Instead, he waited and watched as new speculative longs at other houses entered the market in response to the burgeoning publicity about the silver streak. The Hunts, who had owned substantial physicals and futures since 1974, were assured by counsel that they could not be held as manipulators or market squeezers. Even so, they were not very active on the buy side in October 1979. They had become incensed at the CBOT's rule changes of October 18 limiting their holdings there to no more than six hundred lots in each account, and directing that the reduction be accomplished by February 1980 (later extended to April 1). The Hunts continued to act in good faith. They not only failed to increase their December and March contracts, but actually reduced their outstanding positons on both exchanges during October 1979.

Ironically, few people outside the industry realize that when the Hunts did an EFP with the firm of Ralph Peters, CBOT chairman, in the amount of more than 1,300 lots of silver, they not only reduced the "congestion" in their outstanding long positions, but they also reduced the potential liability of Peters on the short side by an equal number of silver ounces.

In New York the Hunts arranged for EFPs with Mocatta, again lessening their outstanding long positions and reducing the short-side exposure of this aggressive bullion dealer. Many professionals noted the good fortune of Mocatta as the Hunts decided to cooperate and reduce the "congestion" about which that very same bullion dealer had complained.

As October chilled into a stormy November, the silver bulls who held large positions continued to hold them, except those erased by EFPs. It appeared that the restrictive rule changes, together with continuing pressure by federal agencies fearful of an imaginary silver squeeze, would restrain the silver bulls from taking significant new positions.

Action in the silver markets during November continued to resemble the pattern of October. Table IV indicates the price action and the open interest in the two months (December and March) that concerned the exchanges and the federal agencies. Notice that in both contract months the activity seemed fairly normal, with the nearest delivery month (December) encountering the usual decline in open interest.

But while conditions in the silver market appeared deceptively calm, international and domestic events were building a bonfire under American inflation. The major ingredient fueling that fire was OPEC oil.

From the time Americans were once again permitted to own gold bullion, at the end of 1974, the price of gold had been inversely linked to the strength or weakness of the dollar. When the dollar strengthened, gold declined; when the dollar weakened, gold rose. And so it went from early 1975 through most of 1978. But as 1978 trailed to a close, it be-

TABLE IV
SETTLEMENT PRICE/PREV. DAY OPEN INTEREST:
COMEX SILVER—NOV. 1979

Trade Date	Dec. '79 Silver Price	Daily Net Change	Prev. Day Open Int.	Mar. '80 Silver Price	Daily Net Change	Prev. Day Open Int.
1	16.9	−40	12,137	16.96	−40	29,214
2	16.29	−10	12,047	16.84	−12	29,210
5	16.485	+19.5	11,816	17.055	+21.5	29,083
6	16.87	+38.5	12,125	17.45	+39.5	29,117
7	16.75	−12	11,902	17.345	−10.5	29,400
8	16.67	−8	12,125	17.26	−8.5	29,621
9	16.42	−25	11,968	17.025	−23.5	29,894
12	16.39	−3	12,005	17.015	−1	30,047
13	15.99	−40	11,965	16.615	−40	30,623
14	16.27	+28	11,588	16.89	+27.5	30,711
15	16.16	−11	11,333	16.775	−11.5	31,599
16	16.30	+14	11,287	16.925	+15	31,908
19	16.32	+2	11,005	16.95	+2.5	31,739
20	16.30	−2	10,832	16.95	0	31,941
21	16.00	−30	10,212	16.675	−27.5	32,585
23	16.32	+32	9,530	16.995	+32	32,657
26	16.405	+8.5	9,544	17.07	+7.5	32,615
27	16.805	+40	9,243	17.47	+40	32,931
28	18.26	+145.5	8,902	17.87	+40	32,832
29	18.16	−10	7,515	18.47	+60	33,415
30	18.82	+66	2,465	19.27	+80	32,978

came painfully evident to market-watchers that a new fundamental factor had entered the gold equation: the price of a barrel of crude oil. Simply put, if the price of oil rose, then the price of precious metals—gold, silver, platinum—had to rise. And since the prospect of a price decline in oil in 1979 and 1980 appeared unlikely, the corollary became clear: When OPEC raised the price of oil, the markets raised the price of gold.

But throughout October and for three weeks into November the prices of gold and silver traded in a narrow, featureless pattern, some days up, other days down. Unlike the markets of late August and September, there were few limit-up days in November for the December and March Comex silver contracts. Indeed, the limit-down days exceeded the limit-ups by about two-to-one. Changes were shallow on most trading days. At the Chicago and New York silver exchanges certain self-seeking interests chose to ignore that open interest was declining for the near December delivery, and instead made waves about an oncoming "congestion" in the December contract and the threat of a squeeze by the longs. This went on, even though representatives of the holders of the majority long positions in December silver had assured the boards of both exchanges that the positions would be rolled forward, switched to future months, or liquidated by way of EFPs. The exchange boards kept up their pressure on the clearing firms to cause the longs to let go.

While the longs at this point were not buying significantly, neither were they in haste to let go. And to be fair about it, why should they have knuckled under to the boards that had abandoned the market's traditional neutral position in order to make rules favoring the trade shorts rather than remain market neutral?

The explanation is that each metals exchange is presided over by a board of directors that makes and can change rules to prevent trade members from getting financially buried by speculators who have not invested in exchange seats. Juvenal once asked, "Who will guard the guards?" In the case of commodities futures exchanges dominated by trade and floor interests, the rules are made by the guards to guard the guards. By the third week in November the exchange boards in both silver futures cities not only had formulated margin rules designed to stifle public participation in the silver markets, but were preoccupied to an almost maniacal degree with trying to get Norton Waltuch, the other large Conti accounts, and the Hunts to let go of their positions for the obvious benefit of the imperiled shorts.

Some years before moving to the new offices at 4 World Trade Center Mocatta's psychiatrist chairman had a cartoon on a wall near his desk reflecting a rather sensible golden rule: "He who has the gold makes the rules." Evidently this reasoning applied equally well to silver. And since the margin raises decreed by the exchange boards had all but shut out the small speculators and most of the locals from the silver futures market, the open interest on that side of the two-way trade gradually congested into the thin ranks of the bullion dealers. This occurred by the third week of November 1979.

Earlier that month, on November 4, a Sunday, a group of Iranian crazies stormed the United States Embassy in Iran. They overran and occupied the supposedly sacrosanct premises of the diplomatic mission, and captured and held hostage fifty-odd American citizens inside the embassy. On November 5 and 6 silver contracts were bought heavily by speculators who felt that the President would send the Marines to Tehran. But when it became apparent that the Administration was afflicted with analysis paralysis (substitution of study for courage), the enthusiasm of the in-and-out traders waned. Silver went into a decline until Thanksgiving, November 22.

After the holiday recess visible change appeared in the markets. The time approached in November when the December delivery would become the spot month. Some shorts became fearful that the longs would demand delivery rather than liquidate through normal offsetting sales.

On Monday, November 26, spot silver rose by 8.5 cents to $16.405. The open interest for December on November 23 stood at 9,544 contracts, or 47,720,000 ounces. Delivery of all the involved silver in the futures contracts would have required $7.8 billion. By the close of business on November 28, when the value of the spot month settled at $18.26 after a one-day leap of $1.46 per ounce, the open interest in December silver had dropped to 7,515 contracts. By the close of business November 29, when silver for December delivery settled at $18.16, there were only 2,465 contracts open. And on the last trading day of November the December open interest stood at 2,310, a rather small number for any contract month that still had seventeen trading sessions to go before the contract could be wiped off the exchange listing.

Would there be a December squeeze? With a total open interest of 11.5 million ounces, when there were over 55 million ounces sitting in Comex warehouses? As Mr. Goldschmidt told the Comex board back in September, "You don't have a problem."

But evidently some of the board members did. They lost plenty of money on overhedged or naked short positions as the December holders of the longs profited.

So now a hue and cry developed concerning the alarmingly large open positions in the March Comex delivery contracts.

On the last trading day in November the March '80 Comex contract went limit-up as speculative and floor shorts scrambled to cover by buying from the bullion dealers. There were 32,986 March contracts open on that day, and during the first session of Comex trading in December the open interest in the March contract increased slightly to 33,020. Table V delineates the settlement prices of both the December '79 and the March '80 contracts during December 1979, also the constantly decreasing open interest.

Table V
Settlement Price/Prev. Day Open Interest: Comex Silver—Dec. 1979

Trade Date	Dec. '79 Silver Price	Daily Net Change	Prev. Day Open Int.	Mar. '80 Silver Price	Daily Net Change	Prev. Day Open Int.
3	20.05	+123	2,310	20.07	+80	32,986
4	19.78	−27	1,778	20.40	+33	33,020
5	19.542	−23.8	1,390	20.17	−23	32,895
6	19.18	−36.2	986	19.81	−36	32,597
7	18.76	−42	851	19.37	−44	32,804
10	19.16	+40	844	19.80	+43	32,864
11	19.99	+83	753	20.30	+50	32,645
12	20.08	+9	803	20.75	+45	32,155
13	21.00	+92	609	21.50	+75	32,097
14	21.65	+65	687	22.38	+88	31,975
17	22.35	+70	545	23.15	+77	31,837
18	23.70	+135	472	24.15	+100	31,528
19	23.63	−7	511	24.50	+35	31,319
20	23.50	−13	295	24.30	−20	31,620
21	24.35	+85	162	25.055	+75.5	31,089
26	25.50	+120	158	26.05	+99.5	30,732
27			192	27.05	+100	30,883
28				28.05	+100	30,517
31				29.05	+100	30,573

During December several events occurred that spurred interest in precious metals prices, gold as well as silver. The Iranian hostage situation had now deteriorated into a cause célèbre without any ready solution. Two years after Afghanistan had surrendered to the Soviet Union without a fight pockets of revolutionary problems were arising to plague the Soviets, who had installed, for example, the ruble as the country's circulating medium in all the banks. If any businessman were asked to whom does a country belong when the banks use the currency of another country, it wouldn't take two master's degrees in finance to come up with the obvious answer.

Meantime OPEC had commenced another round of oil price hikes. Inflation had risen in the United States to an admitted rate of 13 percent per annum (actually it was closer to 20 percent if only the necessities of life were measured, including meat, flour, and gasoline, let alone bread). By early December practically the entire March '80 open interest on the short side appeared to be held by the bullion dealers, including Mocatta Metals, J. Aron, Philipp Brothers (a division of Engelhard), Sharps, Pixley, etc.

In Lima, Alfredo Fonseca dabbed nervously at his temples as he looked at the silver price. During October he had overhedged at the suggestion of well-meaning brokers in New York, going short some 13 million ounces of silver for December delivery at an average price of $17.85.

As December opened, at the end of the first trading day spot silver stood wavering at $20.05. Figuring round-turn commissions, MINPECO's loss, if it could be covered at the existing price, would exceed $28 million.

But why cover? After all, people who were in the know had advised Fonseca that silver couldn't stay up over $18 an ounce and would most likely work its way back toward the $9 level. All he had to do was hang in there and have MINPECO put up the variation margin. By the end of trading on December 7 the variation margin needed for the account had declined to a mere $11.8 million, and the price of silver seemed to be heading downward.

But something terrible happened.

President Carter ordered a massive flotilla to the Mediterranean, the Indian Ocean, and the Persian Gulf. The Mosque in Mecca, Islam's holiest shrine, was invaded and seized by religious fanatics, possibly with Iranian connections. The American Embassy in Islamabad, capital of Pakistan, was burned and two Americans were killed. In Afghanistan the Soviets, who had already installed two successive puppet regimes, were now having their problems with the current head of that state, later denounced as an agent of the West and executed. It appeared at the time that military intervention in the Persian Gulf was inevitable if the United States wanted to free the hostages and keep the Soviet Union from establishing for itself a trouble-free path from the Khyber Pass to the Indian Ocean, a Russian objective since the days of Peter the Great.

No speculator in his or her right mind would dare go short precious metals in the light of these international uncertainties. But plenty of them wanted to go long. The bullion dealers were called upon again to supply the short side of the market.

As previously mentioned, the bullion dealer cannot undergo excess exposure. The situation in December silver reminded me of the time in January 1958 when AT&T suddenly declared its first increased dividend in twenty-nine years and the first stock split (3 for 1) in its entire history. The price of the telephone company shares was in the neighborhood of $205 at the time the announcement hit the trading floor. So many orders to buy at the market flooded in on the floor that trading was immediately suspended, because no one in his or her right mind would sell AT&T in such a situation—except the specialist in the stock. Trading resumed seventy-five minutes later at $245 a share, and 75,000 shares were sold to the buyers by the specialist. Several days later the market in the phone company shares dipped enough for the specialist to cover and save his skin.

An almost similar situation developed during the second trading week in December. From the tenth through the fourteenth every day saw silver surge higher. It settled on Friday at $21.65, and Fonseca's superiors decided to cover, since they didn't have the silver on hand to make delivery.

On Monday and Tuesday, the seventeenth and eighteenth, silver for December '79 delivery leaped skyward as the bullion dealers accommodated the distress buy orders entered by MINPECO's brokers. When the smoke settled by the end of the week on December 21, the price of December silver settled at $24.35. MINPECO had lost about $80 million, the open interest had been reduced to 158, and the delivery month died peacefully, without any squeeze or corner.

Christmas 1979 proved to be a happy time for all the silver bulls. When the market reopened for the last four trading sessions of the year, the demand by the silver longs became inflamed by the news that the Afghan president, Hafizullah Amin, had been ousted and executed in a coup reportedly supported by Soviet troops.

The "invasion" by Soviet troops into a country that had surrendered to the USSR without a fight gave the American press the kind of news that sells papers and creates diversions in the minds of our citizens from the basic problems created by the Administration. For example, the press seemed very anxious to point out that the primary military lesson to be learned from the Soviet "invasion" of a territory presumably for more than twenty months considered their own was that the Soviets have the ability to move massive numbers of troops in a very brief span of time into areas where they see a threat to their policies.

Mr. Carter and his crew leaped on that lesson like a hungry tuna into a school of milling herring. They took the tack that Soviet success in this exercise would further shift the balance of power in the Middle East and South Asia against the United States.

While the President and his indefatigable advisers belabored how to make political capital out of the Afghanistan fiasco, the March Comex delivery ended the month of December trading with three limit-up sessions, gaining $1 an ounce each day.

Imagine! A future whose former daily limit moves were calculated on a change of 20 cents per ounce now found itself moving daily up $1 an ounce, or five times the former limit. There were more than 30,000 contracts in the March delivery, or 150 million ounces. Every $1 move up meant the bullion dealers who were on the short side had to pony up $150 million a day variation margins to the exchange clearing house. If they were 100 percent hedged—that is, if the outstanding shorts were covered by physicals owned in certified warehouses and hocked at friendly banks—there could be no problem in getting that money, even though the shorts had to pay increasingly high interest rates for its use.

But were all the shorts fully hedged against physicals? And didn't one of the larger shorts face daily increasing exposure from the mark-to-the-market funds that had to be deposited at the custodian banks to protect the holders of the options granted by that bullion dealer?

The March Comex contract ended 1979 at $29.05, almost 50 percent higher than its level at the start of December 1979. A rise of $10 an ounce on 30,000 silver contracts meant deposits of at least $1.5 billion. But at the end of 1979 the increase in equity in the March Comex delivery for the Hunt Group hovered well over $1.2 billion. To be sure, the Hunts did not let this kind of interest-free money lie around idle at their brokers. The funds were put to use to buy securities and other forms of participation in oil and other natural resource enterprises.

The formerly bearish silver advisories and research dispatches now suddenly made a reversal. Market letter writers could foresee the U.S. moving to the brink of war. Who could blame American investors for suddenly rushing to put their inflation-weakened dollars aboard the gold and silver train before it pulled out?

Bank withdrawals to buy Kruggerands and precious metals caused increasing concern at the Federal Reserve. Paul Volcker, the Federal Reserve chairman, who had been criticized for moving too slowly to fight inflation with high interest rates, prepared to act. The GSA had stopped its Treasury gold auctions after December, so the supply of gold was reduced. Retail outlets sprang up by the hundreds offering ready cash for old gold and silver scrap, and the coin shops began to do business at a level never before dreamed or imagined.

In was in this sort of atmosphere that the silver market opened on the London Metal Exchange Wednesday, January 2, while most U.S. citizens were still sleeping. Spot silver traded in the LME ring that morning at 1,690 pence. Some five hours later, when trading opened on the Comex in New York, silver shot up the dollar limit to settle at $30.05. Open interest on the March '80 Comex delivery had declined to 29,370 contracts, which was less than the number of contracts open in the March '79 delivery in January 1979. Would the longs hold out and squeeze the shorts? Mr. Goldschmidt of Conti had assured the Comex directors that it wouldn't happen. The Hunts had given similar assurances in personal visits at the exchanges, at the CFTC, and through letters.

But the Comex board members who were short were evidently not satisfied with such apodictical assurances. They wanted the longs to let go, and the longs were in no hurry.

On January 7, 1980, the special margin committee, chaired by Dr. Jarecki, suggested that the Comex set limits on the number of positions any one trader by himself or in concert with others could hold in any single delivery month. The number proposed and adopted turned out to be five hundred contracts. The Hunts, of course, had far more contracts, and Norton Waltuch and the so-called "foreign investors" also held positions in excess of the proposed five hundred-contract limit. A limit of two thousand contracts in all delivery months was adopted in order not to shut down the New York silver market completely.

Back on October 18 the CBOT had established a six hundred-contract position limit, but the effective date for this limit had been deferred until April 1, 1980, to give the large longs time to roll over some of the positions, and gradually liquidate others by offset or EFPs.

However, on January 7 the Comex board met and adopted "Silver Rule 7," making any account with more than a hundred contracts a reportable account. No individual could carry more than two thousand contracts, counting all his accounts with all member firms, or more than five hundred contracts for any one delivery month. Bona fide hedgers were, as usual, exempted from this rule.

Thus the rule designed to stifle speculation and force the longs to let go would take effect by February 18 and eliminate once and for all any danger of a squeeze on the March delivery.

Since the effective date of Silver Rule 7 happened to be February 18, what did the longs do on January 8? Table VI indicates price action and open interest in the March '80 Comex futures.

Notice that after January 8 there was a brief flurry of selling by some of the smaller longs. But now a strange thing happened in the pits.

Lowell Mintz, chairman of the Comex, reported to the board on January 9 that there was evidence that in the wake of the board's adoption of the restrictive Silver Rule of January 7, the larger longs were apparently buying January and February silver contracts up to the monthly position limit of five hundred, thus creating the possibility of a squeeze on the shorts for those months. At this, one of the commission house board members proposed that the positions in January and February Comex silver be restricted to no more than fifty contracts per account.

TABLE VI
SETTLEMENT PRICE/PREV. DAY OPEN INTEREST:
COMEX SILVER—JAN. 1980

Trade Date	Mar. '80 Silver Price	Daily Net Change	Prev. Day Open Int.	May '80 Silver Price	Daily Net Change	Prev. Day Open Int.
2	30.05	+100	30,356	30.48	+100	21,491
3	31.05	+100	29,370	31.48	+100	20,157
4	32.05	+100	28,634	32.48	+100	19,302
7	33.05	+100	28,116	33.48	+100	18,938
8	32.75	−30	27,568	33.25	−23	17,940
9	33.50	+75	27,803	34.00	+75	17,613
10	34.50	+100	26,865	35.00	+100	17,362
11	35.50	+100	27,238	36.00	+100	17,602
14	36.50	+100	27,193	37.00	+100	17,440
15	37.50	+100	24,930	38.00	+100	17,002
16	38.50	+100	23,869	39.00	+100	16,717
17	39.50	+100	21,798	40.00	+100	15,540
18	40.50	+100	21,507	41.00	+100	15,640
21	41.50	+100	19,263	42.00	+100	15,345
22	40.50	−100	19,172	41.00	−100	15,338
23	39.50	−100	17,983	40.00	−100	15,771
24	38.50	−100	17,302	39.00	−100	12,814
25	37.50	−100	16,445	38.00	−100	12,499
28	36.50	−100	15,458	37.00	−100	12,297
29	37.00	+50	14,148	37.50	+50	12,878
30	36.50	−50	13,225	37.00	−50	12,670
31	35.70	−80	13,060	36.25	−75	12,680

That is why the "emergency" Silver Rule 7 was so amended on January 9, and the proverbial die was now cast to force the longs to let go.

Almost simultaneously, a burst of buying appeared in the London markets. It was rumored that the Hunts and the Saudis were transferring their business from Comex to the LME and that the bullion dealers already short the 27,193 March contracts on January 11 would go belly up because they would not be able to make delivery of the silver if the longs insisted on taking it and continued to support the market by buying LME metal.

In New York, outside the one-day down market on January 8, and a less than limit-up move of 75 cents on January 9, silver had gone limit-up each trading day since the month opened. The bullion dealers who were short had to deposit more than $135 million a day in variation margin—and high interest rates were getting higher. Moreover, with silver at $35 an ounce, no sterling manufacturer or jeweler seemed anxious to buy the metal for inventory. And Eastman Kodak, the largest user of silver in the country, had long since dropped out of the buy side of the silver picture. Without question the bullion dealers were losing a good deal of the physicals business because the market price of the metal had risen to such a lofty level. The growing anxiety of the bullion dealers was evident. So was their determination to make the silver tracks run the other way.

In London on January 14 the silver price appeared to be headed in one direction: up. The metal traded at 1,810 pence for spot, and then moved higher. By January 18 LME purchases had pulled the spot price to an all-time record of 2,150 pence. In New York on Comex the spot January contract traded at $48.80 on Thursday, January 17, and then dropped a bit to close on Friday at $46.80. Ordinarily the bullion dealers provide fine silver to the trade to be formed into alloys and used for a multitude of practical purposes. But at those levels the market for spot silver simply died.

About a year earlier Dr. Jarecki had described the silver market as a heroine placed on the track by a villain (the longs). Would she be saved? He assured his readers that the "heroine" is usually rescued at the last minute. But in January time and the realities of the silver market seemed to give a dangerous edge to the speeding train.

Market rules limited daily price moves for future months to $1 an ounce, but did not apply to the current, or spot (January), delivery. On one day, from January 16 to January 17, the price of spot silver shot up by $3.10 an ounce, to $48.80. Nominally, the settlement price for the March and May contracts moved up their limits, but what resulted was an anomaly: future deliveries selling for much less than spot silver. The clearinghouse members were realistic. They pegged the future delivery months at a differential above the spot month, and demanded that their short customers pay variation margins based on the higher prices, not on the artificially pegged settlement price, which was $39.50 for the March contract. The train was whistling in the distance, and the question was whether the shorts could rescue the fettered silver market.

Added to the distress of the silver shorts were the woes heaped upon them inadvertently by the President.

On NBC's "Meet the Press," Sunday, January 20, President Carter proposed a boycott of the summer Moscow Olympics. He opposed sending an American Olympic team to Moscow while Soviet troops were in Afghanistan. The President apparently wished to present himself as too busy with foreign crises to bother about such domestic problems as gold at $850 an ounce and silver at $50. He also, with less than total success, appeared to be holding himself out to the world, including American voters, as a strong decisive leader.

On the day after this Presidential appearance, the Comex board held an emergency meeting at 8:00 A.M. Monday, January 21, to decide whether to act to dampen speculation in gold futures. At the meeting the board raised to $15,000 the initial margin for one gold contract.

But the Comex board members did not leave for their offices when the gold meeting ended. At nine a special meeting on the silver situation convened. The chairman noted that the large longs continued to maintain a goodly portion of the world's silver supply. He ran on to point out that even though position limits were set by Comex on January 7, the open interest had not been materially reduced (actually, the March open interest had been reduced by almost 30 percent). The longs continued to buy in order to take delivery.

Someone then suggested that the board limit trades to liquidation only, to get the longs to let go. But first the board had to declare whether an emergency situation existed. Even though this was not the case, the Comex board resolved that an emergency existed because of significant concentrations that could cause the March maturity and other maturities to fail to liquidate in a normal fashion.

Therefore, the board postponed opening the market until 11:30 A.M. (Comex silver normally opens for trading at 9:50 A.M.).

The ensuing discussion ran past 11 A.M., and the board further postponed the silver market opening to 12:30 P.M.

Then the board recessed.

When the meeting resumed, the discussion focused on the level of silver margins. The time for the silver opening was moved yet again, to 1:30 P.M.

The Comex attorney then summarized the proceedings, a motion was made, seconded, and carried to make silver trading for liquidation only. The action that finally saved the "heroine" was taken—in the nick of time as in the old films.

In his State of the Union message on January 23, Jimmy Carter warned the Soviet Union that he would use military force if necessary to protect the Persian Gulf. Such a speech might have added several dollars to the silver price, but there could be no new buying by anybody, except shorts who were liquidating. The longs had no place to go, no normal market to absorb their holdings. They found themselves now locked in perilously by the Comex rules—rules formulated by a board including at least four members representing firms that held the major portion of the shorts in all the outstanding open interests.

The longs had no one to sell to, except those firms that had open shorts, firms that had helped to make the self-serving Silver Rule 7.

The liquidation rule on Comex, coupled with the liquidation and position-limit rules on both Comex and CBOT, caused consternation to foreign firms, who were accustomed to arbitrage between LME silver and the futures on American exchanges. While in London on January 21 silver traded steadily at 2,150 pence for spot metal, the spot month in New York on Comex presented one of the wildest swinging markets ever seen in silver trading. High for the trading session on January 21 in January silver was $49. Low was $37, and the contract closed at $44.

But from that day on the silver price went downhill. The January silver contract went off the boards a few days later at $33.95. On the last trading day in January the March Comex contract settled for $35.70, with 13,060 contracts open.

The first day of February trading activity on Comex found the March silver contract under pressure, supposedly because the longs had no place to go. But evidently they did have plenty of monetary muscle at the time, because they allowed the word to get around that they would not liquidate their positions, but instead would demand delivery and pay in cash.

At the end of the first day of trading in February, the March delivery open interest stood at 12,757 contracts of 5,000 ounces each. The settlement price on this future at the end of trading that day turned out to be $33.75, or a limit-down move of $1 an ounce from the previous close. Obviously, the price the next day and the next and the next should have collapsed limit-down as the longs let go. But it is an unwritten rule that the silver market never does what the experts think it will do. Table VII shows the action in the March contract during February.

Notice that instead of collapsing, the silver price went limit-up for the next five trading sessions, through February 11. Were the longs buying more contracts? They couldn't do this because of the board's liquidation-only order. So obviously the buying had to come from the shorts, who were closing out some of their positions. And naturally the longs had an opportunity to offset their precarious contracts on the shorts if this were the case. But even though there were five sessions in a row of limit-up trading in March silver, the open interest declined by less than two thousand contracts during the rise. On Lincoln's Birthday help came for the shorts from an unlikely source: the Federal Reserve Board.

The Board's interest in the course of the gold and silver prices was nothing new. A former member of the Board had in fact headed the so-called Silver Committee, formed of Comex members who were supposedly "disinterested" in matters pertaining to silver. The committee had been carefully chosen to fulfill a public relations function, since its only member familiar with the metals markets was Oscar Burchard, president of Ore & Chemical, a close friend of Henry Jarecki, who could hardly be called "disinterested" in the silver market.

While this committee obviously had been the link between Comex and the Federal Reserve Board, its real duties—to monitor the market and establish margins and rules to keep the market fair and orderly—had been taken over in December 1979 by a special margin committee chaired, of course, by Dr. Jarecki. And it was on the information and suggestions supplied to the Comex board by this committee that the Board made the decision to establish the liquidation-only rule. This rule, of course, was designed to break the silver price and benefit the trade member shorts.

But the restrictive rules might never have resulted in the

TABLE VII
SETTLEMENT PRICE/PREV. DAY OPEN INTEREST: COMEX SILVER—FEB. 1980

Trade Date	Mar. '80 Silver Price	Daily Net Change	Prev. Day Open Int.	May '80 Silver Price	Daily Net Change	Prev. Day Open Int.
1	34.75	-95	12,724	35.25	-100	12,598
4	33.75	-100	12,754	34.25	-100	12,526
5	34.75	+100	12,264	35.25	+100	12,456
6	35.75	+100	12,405	36.25	+100	11,269
7	36.75	+100	11,578	37.25	+100	11,169
8	37.75	+100	11,775	38.25	+100	11.193
11	38.75	+100	11,625	39.25	+100	10,785
12	38.60	-15	10,779	39.25	0	10,714
13	37.60	-100	10,727	38.30	-95	10,630
14	36.60	-100	10,434	37.45	-85	10,594
15	36.00	-60	10,416	36.85	-60	10,416
19	35.00	-100	9,458	35.85	-100	10,529
20	34.00	-100	9,011	34.85	-100	10,503
21	34.70	+70	8,462	35.50	+65	10,805
22	33.70	-100	8,196	34.50	-100	11,147
25	34.00	+30	7,026	34.95	+45	11,578
27	33.70	-30		34.59	-36	
28	35.20	+150	5,260	35.34	+75	11,823
29	35.30	+10	2,353	36.34	+100	12,009

silver price collapse that came in March if the Federal Reserve had not made waves about banks and their loans to bullion hoarders like the Hunts, and if interest rates had not been twisted up sharply by the Fed.

The government's harsh attitude toward gold and silver loans, together with the effect of credit controls and rising interest rates established to try to control a malignant inflation, put a severe crimp in the plans of the longs to stand for delivery and to finance any silver so delivered.

Much of the silver had already been delivered during December and had been transported abroad. Swiss interest rates have always been lower than those in the U.S. or Great Britain. And loans at 6 to 6½ percent were much more palatable to silver hoarders than paying several percentage points above the prime of 15¾ percent. Indeed, so much silver had flowed into the vaults in Zurich that expansion plans had to be implemented by the busy Swiss banks, whose operations historically have promised secrecy and security for depositors and users of bank services. These services include buying and selling commodity futures all over the world.

Now the holders of the long side of the March Comex silver open interest had little room to maneuver. They could hardly roll their holdings over to May or later months because the spreads had become economically unrealistic. They could not accept much silver for delivery by remaining long until the end of the month because they could not finance the silver sensibly, and because of the Fed's stringent credit controls. They could only liquidate through offset—and the accommodating buyers were the trade member shorts.

On Monday, February 19, the spot month (February) on which prices could move without limit dropped $4.80 an ounce to $31. The open interest dropped by more than a thousand contracts as the longs locked into the March contract switched into the spot month (February) and took it on the chin for the differential. By the time February ended and March became the spot month, the open interest in the March contract had dwindled to about 2,057 contracts.

Obviously, there would be no squeeze on the March delivery month positions. Like the September and December 1979 deliveries, the March Comex contract seemed destined to go off the boards in a normal, orderly fashion, without squeeze or corner. But with the market biased in favor of the shorts, they stood to make millions during the descent that led to Silver Thursday.

On the first trading day in March silver stood staunchly at $35.20 for the spot month on Comex. While the entire world of market-watchers and market participants believed that the basic direction of silver was downward because of the restrictive exchange trading rules, the margin levels and position restrictions were such as to discourage speculators who might otherwise have leaped in great numbers on the short side of the market. Moreover, the market was constantly subjected to crosscurrents of opinion based on the question of who held the silver.

At this point the press had published so much on the silver market that the longs had been categorized into two distinct camps: (1) the Hunts, and (2) Norton Waltuch's "foreign accounts" at Conti. The media and experts alike realized that the Hunts controlled vast wealth and resources. And the implication that the Conti accounts represented the oil wealth of the Middle East, Saudi Arabia in particular, went far to deter new shorts from piling on the obvious silver slide. The Comex, on January 8, amended its liquidation-only rule as it noticed that the longs were unable to find adequate financing for open positions because of Federal credit restrictions.

During the first week in March the Comex spot month declined about 10 percent from $35.20 to $32.90. But the following week the prime rate rose to 20 percent. President Carter made his pitch about the profligacy of consumers, whom he blamed for inflation the government actually

TABLE VIII
SETTLEMENT PRICE/PREV. DAY OPEN INTEREST:
COMEX SILVER—MARCH 1980

Trade Date	Mar. '80 Silver Price	Daily Net Change	Prev. Day Open Int.	May '80 Silver Price	Daily Net Change	Prev. Day Open Int.
3	35.20	-10	2,057	35.98	-36	12,168
4	36.15	+95	1,874	36.85	+87	12,184
5	36.05	-10	1,422	36.80	-5	12,687
6	33.10	-295	1,120	36.05	-75	11,667
7	32.90	-20	892	35.05	-100	12,703
10	29.75	-315	903	34.05	-100	12,620
11	29.10	-65	1,136	33.05	-100	12,695
12	29.30	+20	1,016	32.05	-100	12,449
13	25.50	-380	981	31.05	-100	12,535
14	21.00	-450	1,231	30.05	-100	12,255
17	17.40	-360	1,892	29.05	-100	12,180
18	17.80	+40	2,588	28.05	-100	11,484
19	20.55	+275	2,363	27.05	-100	11,254
20	22.35	+180	2,058	26.05	-100	10,831
21	22.50	+15	1,315	25.05	-100	10,630
24	21.25	-125	927	24.05	-100	10,599
25	20.20	-105	552	23.05	-100	10,318
26	15.80	-440	416	22.05	-100	9,664
27				21.05	-100	9,100
28				20.05	-100	8,756
31				19.05	-100	8,088

caused. The price of silver collapsed about 30 percent in five trading sessions to stand at $21 an ounce at the end of trading on March 14. (See Table VIII.)

It was at this time that the Hunts began to explore seriously the feasibility of floating silver-backed bonds on the stockpile they had accumulated. This actually set the stage for a day that will go down in business history as Silver Thursday.

SIX

*

SILVER THURSDAY

At seventy Charles ("Charley") Mattey has been in the commodity business for more than fifty years and has risen to executive vice president at Bache Halsey Stuart Shields, the nation's second-ranking brokerage firm after Merrill Lynch. Little did he ever dream that Bache would totter on the brink of bankruptcy because a sudden drop in the price of silver affected the holdings of a major customer of the firm.

Nor in early 1980 could many Wall Street savants foresee the day when a change in the price of silver could cause tremors through the entire stock market and adversely affect, at least temporarily, the reputations for financial soundness carefully constructed for ages by leading brokerage and commodity firms.

Nor could any market-watcher ever envision the day when Merrill Lynch, Bache, and the New York Stock Exchange would petition the CFTC actually to close the silver markets because of a threat they supposedly posed to the nation's financial structure.

Yet all of these things happened, and more, on March 27, 1980, the day that came to be known as Silver Thursday.

Silver Thursday, of course, did not actually begin on March 27. The background for the selling climax that occurred on that date began many months earlier, certainly no later than January 1980.

On January 1, 1980, the Hunts and their corporate allies controlled over 192 million ounces of silver in physical metal, options, futures contracts, and forward contracts. Their positions were divided as follows:

Nelson Bunker Hunt	79,028,000 ounces
William Herbert Hunt	47,569,000 ounces
IMIC	61,873,000 ounces
Hunt International	774,900 ounces
Planet	3,000,000 ounces
Total	192,244,900 ounces

For every drop of $1 in the price of silver the equity of this massive position declined more than $192 million. And, of course, for every dollar of rise in the silver price the value of the holdings rose $192 million.

The Hunts have always been quite friendly with Bache management, a venerable old brokerage house founded by Jules Bache in the nineteenth century and later headed by his nephew Harold Bache for many years before it absorbed other firms and added new names to its title. Charley Mattey, current dean of commodity traders and futures industry executives in New York, has always lived by the credo that the customer normally comes first, but when the chips are down, the company comes before everything else.

In early January, when it was evident that Comex intended to change the rules of the futures ball game, the way out for the Hunts and some of the other large longs was simply to switch their futures into physicals, hock the physicals abroad at interest rates, which were of course tax deductions, and shift their future forward buying, if any, to the London Metal Exchange.

Bache, of course, has a London subsidiary that deals in physical metals. Because silver, in early January, was on the rise, it was not too difficult for Bache to accommodate the Hunts with ready financing for their silver stockpile. And even when silver began its gradual descent, the Hunts, with the help of Bache and other friendly brokers, managed to hang on to their hoard. On the last trading day in December 1979 spot silver nudged $35 an ounce. The value of the Hunt silver holdings at year-end approximated $4.7 billion.

In a Congressional inquiry that followed Silver Thursday the Hunts maintained that their silver had cost them less than $10 an ounce, on average; their year-end '79 holdings represented an increase in equity of $2.7 billion. Also, the Hunts had other collateral than silver futures, physicals, coins, and options. They had securities and investments in energy that ran into the billions of dollars. In retrospect, it became clear that the Hunts got into trouble by doing Bache a favor.

Among the securities the Hunts had purchased with money generated by their rising silver equity was a substantial stake in the brokerage firm where they conducted their main silver business: Bache Halsey Stuart Shields. The Hunt purchase, urged upon them by the Bache chairman, appeared to be a good investment, in part because the Hunts pay out in commissions more than any other people on earth. The purchase also helped Bache to stave off, at least for the time, an unwelcome takeover attempt by investors named Belzberg from Toronto.

Bache arranged for silver loans for the Hunts, and in doing so may have endangered the firm's own capital, for

95

the price of silver declined during most of March, and the Hunts, who had shifted their emphasis from futures to physicals during January, could not readily meet the daily variation margins required to maintain their collateralized silver.

On January 1, 1980, Bunker Hunt held 12,556 long March Comex silver contracts, and his brother Herbert held 651 long for the same delivery. In all probability these positions had been liquidated by offset or rolled over via switching before March 3, 1980. So it can be safely assumed that the Hunts took substantial profits on the more than 66 million ounces that disappeared from their accounts before the March Comex contract went off the boards. If the cost basis was actually under $10 for this position, then the Hunts must have realized a gross profit of $1.64 billion.

Buoyed by this success, one can understand the alacrity with which the Hunts entered the physicals market. Since interest rates were rising, one can further understand Bache's desire to help finance their friendly customers who had made an illiquid investment in Bache stock.

Under normal circumstances an owner who sells securities listed for trading on the New York Stock Exchange has to wait about five days to receive a check from his broker. But the Hunts' vast purchases of Bache stock made them owners of more than 5 percent of the issued and outstanding shares, and therefore "insiders." An insider cannot normally dispose of his entire holding at once, but must sell only a small fraction of the holdings on a monthly basis unless he seeks and is granted SEC approval for disposal by secondary offering. Thus the millions that the Hunts had invested in Bache stock were illiquid. Moreover, such securities in a margin account become valueless if the SEC suspends the issue from trading.

So when Bache sent the Hunts a margin call for $100 million on March 26, there was no way the Hunts could use their Bache stock to finance part of the call. Besides, Bunker Hunt was not at home in Dallas. He had gone to Paris, and there, on March 25, the day before Bache issued its margin call, he had announced plans for an unorthodox scheme to issue about $2 billion in bonds backed by the Hunt silver holdings.

It is difficult to sit in judgment on a person's actions, especially when one has never been cast in the role of that person or shared his special circumstances. But why Bunker Hunt chose that precise time to announce a possible offshore flotation of bonds backed by silver is puzzling to a professional. In the first place, such an announcement signaled to the financial world that while the Hunts were loaded with silver, they were obviously short of cash. This suggested a coming liquidity crisis and struck both fear and wonder into the hearts of the brokerage firms and banks holding the Hunts' collateralized loans.

In the second place, the announcement gave some credence to the theory that the Hunts had acted in concert with other major bulls in the accumulation of silver futures and silver physicals, even when there had been no overt link between their buying and that of the Hunts.

The so-called silver-backed bonds were to be issued in various denominations and distributed through large European banks to offshore investors. The Hunts' associates in the venture—those pooling their silver holdings with the Hunts to back the proposed bonds—read like a Who's Who of the Arab world's silver bulls: Prince Faisal Ben Abdulla al Saoud of the Saudi royal family; Sheik Mohammed Al Amoudi of Saudi Arabia; Mahmoud Fustok, a naturalized Saudi of Lebanese origin, whose sister reportedly was once married to a member of the royal family; and Naji Nahas, a Lebanese financier operating from Sao Paolo, Brazil, and Geneva, Switzerland.

But the intimation that the Saudis and the Hunts had purchased silver in concert to gobble up and "corner" the above-ground silver supply paled beside the realization that the Hunts were strapped for cash. Their physical position on March 25, the last trading day for the March future, represented practically their entire silver holdings; because, as we already have surmised, the Hunts had liquidated their outstanding futures contracts before the last delivery day in March, and had converted practically their entire holdings— except for some options granted by Naji Nahas—into physical silver stored at various warehouses and banks. They had also some forward contracts on the LME.

Thus, in the very short space of three days the market was hit by three shocking developments. First came the news of the Hunts' planned silver bond sale. Then followed the news of Bache's $100 million margin call on the Hunts, and then the rumor that the Hunts would be unable to meet the call. Then, on March 27 Al Brodsky, a Comex member acting for Bache and the Hunt interests, began selling, and panic hit the pits. The panic quickly spread.

The first and most pervasive fear involved the terrifying possibility that the Hunts would have to dump all of their securities holdings to pay for the margin calls at Bache and other brokers. The second fear involved the possibility that the Hunts' deficits at the commodity clearing firms would cause those firms to fail and default at the banks and clearinghouses.

The combined commodity exchange in New York's World Trade Center is barely a quarter of a mile from the New York Stock Exchange. News travels with the speed of light, and panic is scarcely slower.

When news of the massive silver selling reached the stock market, the reaction was instantaneous. The Dow Jones Industrial Average, the most widely followed index in the stock market, plummeted twenty-five points. Trading was halted in Bache stock, and was not resumed until April 4. Trading was also halted briefly on the stock of two other publicly held brokerage houses—Dean Witter Reynolds and Shearson Loeb Rhoades, and rumors were rife in Wall Street that other firms, including Paine Webber and even mighty Merrill Lynch, were having capital problems because of the sudden drop in silver's price in March, which reduced the value of the long positions in physicals and futures held for the accounts of the silver bulls.

Bache, Merrill Lynch, and the New York Stock Exchange sent a message to the CFTC asking the Commission to halt trading in silver, presumably to keep the panic from spreading further, but the CFTC denied the request. Spot silver stood at $10.80 an ounce, a drop of about $4.00 from the previous day's close.

As the day wore on, the news spread that with the help of Paul Volcker of the Federal Reserve, a bail-out loan for $1.1 billion had been arranged for the Hunts to help them solve their temporary difficulties, and to prevent the very fabric of American finance from tearing apart. The Dow recovered most of its losses, and trading at the New York Stock Exchange ended the day on a note of confidence.

Why did the government's top banker suddenly do a flip-flop so reminiscent of his boss and come to the rescue of the very type of speculators who had been the target of a squeeze in the credit crunch? How could Volcker favor an individual speculator in the same manner in which the government favored the Chrysler Corporation, a giant auto company that employs thousands?

Strangely enough, Mr. Volcker assented to the granting of a loan to the Placid Oil Corporation if the Hunts would deposit their silver holdings in the corporation and promise not to speculate further in silver. To be sure, Mr. Volcker's interest in aiding the Hunts to achieve liquidity and pay off their deficits had to be endorsed by the White House. And just as clearly, the concern of Mr. Volcker and the White House went far beyond the Hunts.

While the CFTC for many months pursued the Banque Populaire in a vain attempt to learn the names of the forty-five foreign risk-takers it represented in the silver market, the identities of the largest group of silver holders after the Hunts were quite well known. They were Saudi Arabians who were closely linked to, if not acting as agents for, the Saudi royal family.

Mahmoud Fustok, Naji Nahas, and Sheik Aboud Al Amoudi, a Jidda real estate investor, are close to Prince

99

Faisal, the son of Prince Abdullah, third in line for the Saudi throne and commander of that country's national guard. Some well-placed Saudis believed that the silver buying by Fustok, Nahas, and their close associates had to be on behalf of Prince Abdullah, Prince Faisal, and others of the Saudi royal family.

It is no secret that the Saudis have become increasingly irritated with U.S. efforts to persuade them to resist OPEC's oil price hawks. They have also been concerned about the deterioration of the U.S. dollar, in which many of their investments are denominated. What would happen, then, if these powerful oil men suffered a major financial setback in the U.S. silver market? This question, rather than the financial fate of the Texas billionaires, may have led to Paul Volcker's concern with the silver market.

On March 28 the Hunt silver stockpile stood at almost 102 million ounces, and their physicals and LME forward positions through their associated corporations were about 39 million ounces.

If the Hunts, strapped for cash, had been forced to dump this 141 million ounces of silver on the market, there can be little doubt that silver would have dropped below $5 an ounce—this despite Dr. Jarecki's claim that he had formed a consortium of bullion dealers and banks to buy all the silver offered at the $10 level.

In retrospect, one can only wonder what oil price hikes the Saudi Arabians might have approved in the spring and summer of 1980 had they suffered major losses in a silver market debacle.

Silver Thursday created plenty of headlines and pictures of the Fed chairman puffing cigars, and of Congressional committees seeking to find out why silver went from $6 in January 1979 to $50 in January 1980, then cascaded to $10.80 on Silver Thursday before recovering.

No sooner did the market in silver stabilize above $11 an ounce at the end of March and rebound toward the $17 level than the headline-making silver investigations began.

First, a House Committee headed by Congressman Benjamin Rosenthal determined to find out whether the Hunts had acted in concert with each other and with the silver bulls at Conti, in Saudi Arabia, and elsewhere in the world to get control of all the above-ground silver. The committee further wanted to establish whether the silver bulls had hoped to hold up users in the U.S. and elsewhere by doing with silver what OPEC had done with oil.

Naturally the Congressman first summoned the longs. The inquiry began with Bunker and Herbert Hunt. When they told the Congressman they were "too busy" to come to Washington and appear before his committee, he threatened to cite them for contempt. They came. And their testimony reflects, of course, the whole truth and nothing but, as told by the Hunts.

In their "confessions" the estimable gentlemen from Texas managed to convey the impression that they approached trading and accumulating silver "not in concert"; that silver itself was hardly worth discussing between them; and that their primary interest lay in energy, not metals.

Having testified in this matter, the Hunts returned to Texas from Washington to await the call of other committees. Meanwhile, a former employee of theirs vented his obvious spleen by telling the world that silver was always the first order of the day for the Hunts, that they knew precisely how much they were buying and selling, and what it was worth, and, in short, that what they told Congressman Rosenthal's committee could not pass a lie detector test.

This aroused the sensation-seekers in the media to cry out "perjury."

In the meantime, a great ground swell of public resentment about Mr. Volcker's backing of the $1.1 billion Hunt "bail-out" loan caused Senator Proxmire to hold a hearing of the Senate Banking Committee. And, of course, another Senator (Stewart) had to hold a Senate hearing into the alleged hanky-panky in the silver market to make sure the Senate got the same courtesies from the same witnesses that

Congressman Rosenthal's House Committee had already received.

And so the Hunts began practically to commute between Dallas and Washington to give testimony to Congressional committees.

In similar vein the officials at Conti, including Walter Goldschmidt, chairman; Norton Waltuch, vice president; and the attorneys for both the grain company and its subsidiary were also subjected to grillings from the various Congressional committees.

It is ironical that the investigations focused only on the actions of the silver longs rather than the silver shorts. Only in Senator Proxmire's hearings did an inkling emerge of the role the shorts had played in the rise and fall of the silver price. At that hearing it became evident that the congestion in silver happened to be not just on the long side, but even more on the short side.

It is true that as the price of silver kept rising during the months from September to January, the outstanding open interest—always a two-sided affair, remember—became concentrated into the accounts of silver longs such as the Hunts, the Conti accounts, and the Banque Populaire Swiss accounts. Reason for this is that the other speculating silver longs had long ago let go at profits or losses, depending on their entry price into the long side of the silver futures market.

But ever since October 1979 the short side of these long positions had of necessity been supplied by the bullion dealers, who were Comex members. Yet no agency accused the shorts of "squeezing" the longs, or of being a major cause of "congestion" of the silver open interest, because the words "congestion" and "squeeze" apply only to longs. These are the interests who have risked their money in an attempt to make the shorts deliver the silver or else pay up to settle their speculative—and not hedged—contracts. Of course, if the shorts actually had been 100 percent hedged, that is, if they had had delivery grade silver available for every ounce sold short on Comex or CBOT, then they could never have been squeezed by the longs, and there could never have been any danger.

In a subsequent *Fortune* issue (August 11, 1980), whose cover bore the pictures of Bunker and Herbert with the caption: "The Hunts Talk," there is plenty of material pointing to the actions of the shorts, including Mocatta Metals and its chairman, Dr. Henry Jarecki.

Whether or not such frank journalism will lead federal agencies to investigate the accounts and the activities of the short-sellers in silver, who were members of the boards of directors of the involved silver exchanges, is a moot subject. But certainly insights of this nature have to help the attorneys who will probably press lawsuits against these worthies to recover losses suffered when silver collapsed during March 1980.

While it is to be hoped that the silver investigations by Congressional committees may have already blown over, the vestiges of such headline-making events still remain—and cause continuing tremors.

Fairchild Publications, whose magazines include *American Metal Market,* a respected trade journal, ran a series of yellow journalism articles about the Hunt "puzzle." The writer suggested that there seemed to be a connection between the Hunts and certain Congressmen, Larry McDonald of Georgia, and Steve Symms, of Idaho.

The articles mentioned the Hunts' contributions to the campaigns of both Congressmen's campaigns, and explained in rather boring detail how Congressman McDonald managed to help defeat the bill to sell a portion of the remaining 139.5 million-ounce silver stockpile.

In a separate article on Steve Symms the Fairchild people revealed that Symms had traded in silver and made money in silver futures (some $9,600 in 1979). But on balance he had wound up the year losing about $8,000. Since Congressman Symms had managed to lose this money by making his own trading decisions, the article ran on to conclude that he no longer traded his own account but maintained a small discretionary account at Conti managed by Paul Sarnoff. What the newspaper, of course, failed to reveal was how much of the loss the Congressman had recovered via switching account managers.

Concomitant with the articles in the *American Metal Market* the Gannett newspapers ran a series of articles implying that it was a conflict of interest for a politician from the nation's leading silver state to dabble in the products of that state. Here again one can only question the motives for these articles. They not only attempted to link the involved people with the Hunts, but also attempted to picture them as doing something sleazy or unethical. And since many Americans still follow Will Rogers's dictum: "All I know is what I read in the papers," chances are that many people are convinced the Hunts and the others involved in being long silver during the so-called "silver situation" conspired together to buy up, store, and hold on to most of the available silver so that the silver users in America and abroad would be compelled some day to pay higher prices.

Assuredly neither the federal agencies nor the media have finished with the silver situation and its larger players. For one thing, the CFTC is still gathering information for possible future action, or inaction. The Securities and Exchange Commission will probably hold investigative hearings to learn why such brokerage firms as Bache, Paine Webber, Merrill Lynch, A. G. Edwards, et alia were almost imperiled by the collapse of a commodity price during March 1980.

There could also be repercussions from the Proxmire hearings that might cause the trade shorts who made millions on the silver price collapse during March to divulge their profitable activities. Although the Senate Banking Committee may not be the instigator of such revelations, the CFTC may become interested enough to compel such disclosures.

Finally, there are the courts of law, where all the dirty laundry in the silver wars in the pits may finally be washed clean. As Carl Sandburg once wrote, everything, eventually, goes to the lawyers.

For the Hunts, however, the silver venture became a long nightmare. They were exposed to a variety of charges, from manipulation of the markets to unconscionable behavior for hoarding an "essential" metal.

For months prior to Silver Thursday Bunker Hunt had basked in the kind of publicity that comes to a self-made successful entrepreneur. But what happened after the media sank its poison-pen fangs into the silver story turned out to be something else.

*

SEVEN

*

THE
SILVERED
HUNTS

In the backwash of Silver Thursday Nelson Bunker Hunt
and his brother William Herbert were stung by a wave of
publicity portraying them as "silver bunglers," suggesting
that Lamar Hunt, a brother who busies himself mainly with
sports enterprises, had to "hock his Rolex" and that Bunker
had to hock his vast silver coin collection. The respected
Economist of London ran a story headlined "Bunkered." To
help correct some of the misunderstandings and errors in
the media, the Hunts hired a high-priced public relations
firm, Hill and Knowlton, to advise them.

The reports that much of the Hunt property was tied up
as security for debts was not too wide of the mark. The Hunt-
owned Placid Oil Company granted a $1.1 billion loan to the
brothers so that they could settle up the deficits at various

firms in the commodities and securities industry. To get the loan the Hunts had to collateralize practically everything they owned of a personal nature. This, of course, is no more demanding than the terms of any other personal loan made at a local bank by a borrower.

In addition, the media leaped on the Hunts and caricaturized them as fools who lost so much money in silver that they could no longer pose as "billionaires." Nothing could be further from the truth.

On April 23, 1980, I happened to be a speaker on precious metals at the Financial Analysts Federation in Houston, Texas. During an interview at the *Houston Chronicle* I pointed out that future competition with the USSR in the silver market all depends on how badly the Soviet Union will need silver in the next five years. I also pointed out that I consider Bunker Hunt a patriot, since as long as an American had the silver it couldn't fall into the Soviet stockpile. It was a personal pleasure to run on and say: "Bunker Hunt is not a villain, as the papers and magazines made him out to be. . . ."

Evidently neither are his two brothers, W. Herbert and Lamar.

But who really are the Hunts? How did they come to latch onto silver in the first place? And why did they go through so much personal exposure and vilification after providing silver traders and speculators the opportunity to make killings on both the rise and the collapse of the silver price in the short space of about seven months?

In the beginning there arose in Dallas a legendary oilman who ran an inheritance of $5,000 into several billions of dollars worth of oil and gas properties. After H. L. Hunt passed away in 1974, his heirs, who inherited not only the tangibles, but also the father's spirit of free enterprise, increased the residue after probate into perhaps the largest family fortune in America. In addition to holdings in energy enterprises, the Hunts have vast real estate holdings, are the nation's largest producers of beet sugar—and, among other interesting activities, own about four hundred pizza parlors. The most visible—and most talked about—of H. L.'s progeny is Nelson Bunker Hunt (affectionately and otherwise known simply as "Bunker").

Undoubtedly Bunker and his family, which includes nine other H. L. children from two marriages, will eventually be subjects of biographies, autobiographies, perhaps even movies. But Hunt-watchers have estimated that Placid Oil, controlled by family trusts set up in 1935, brings in about $1 million a day, for starters.

Paul Getty, many years ago was asked, "How did you get your start toward making a billion?" And his answer was "I started with a father who had a million."

Nelson and his brothers began their business careers in the shadow of a very dynamic entrepreneur, who maintained almost a mania for secrecy about his affairs and dealings.

Armed with the fortunes left by their father, the Hunt brothers can hardly be blamed for hungering to explore business ventures on their own. Lamar decided to specialize in financing sports enterprises, and became owner of the Kansas City Chiefs professional football franchise, and World Tennis Competition. William H. (known as Herbert) looked after the family's oil and exploration interests.

Bunker worked at first with Herbert, but decided to get into some exciting new areas that made money, including horses. Today Bunker owns or controls over a thousand thoroughbreds and is constantly adding to the string. He became interested in horses not because of the corny reason that his family hails from Texas, but because thoroughbred horses originated in Arabia, an area containing oil.

When the Arab-Israeli conflict erupted in the fall of 1973, Bunker knew the price of oil had to rise. He also knew his family vended each day innumerable gallons of a precious natural resource that immediately became converted into paper money. Bunker and his family had the ability to see twenty years down the road and realize that the purchasing power of paper dollars could go only one way: down. So it is understandable that Bunker searched for a natural asset to replace the one sold by the Hunts, which over a period of time would appreciate in value despite inflation.

Although Dallas is a large city, it would be difficult to imagine that purveyors of securities, commodity figures, and physicals would not approach prospective customers whose income was reputed to exceed $1 million a day. Among those purveyors were the Dials.

The first time I met Scott Dial was at the December 1978 convention of the Northwest Miners Association annual meeting in Spokane, Washington. A tall, intense young man, flashily dressed in western clothes, and dripping Indian silver decorations from head to toe, Scott reached out and gave me his card. It was a piece of silverlike metal, the size and shape of a business card, with the words engraved on it: Scott Dial/Silver. Scott and his brother Mark are third-generation Dallas silver bulls. Their father, Don Dial, happened to be Bunker Hunt's roommate at Culver Military Academy. He later entered the brokerage business with Bache.

Bunker got his baptism in silver from Don Dial and he began doing business with Bache. So when hostilities erupted in the Middle East in 1973 and OPEC put through its first big price hike, Bunker became convinced that the natural asset that could properly replace the oil being depleted from the Hunt reserves had to be silver.

On a trip to the Middle East in 1975 to buy horses, Bunker spent some time with Prince Abdullah of the Saudi royal family. Since the Saudis have always been paid for their oil in dollars, Bunker suggested, logically enough, that Abdullah swap horseflesh for something that would appreciate over the years rather than lose purchasing power. He made a deal to buy horses and deliver silver in payment.

This arrangement was especially attractive to Bunker, since he had begun to build his stockpile of silver by accepting delivery of roughly 40 million ounces from Mocatta in February 1974. Mocatta was short about 35 million ounces, but managed to make delivery and thus avoid a squeeze. Dr. Jarecki, who directed Mocatta's fortunes at that time, must have bitten his cuticles to the bone until the threat of a squeeze ended with the deliveries from the hoard of the Bank of Mexico.

For years thereafter Bunker sat stiffed in with physicals that cost from $3 to $6 an ounce while the markets traded well below those levels. Of course there were compensating factors in owning, storing, and perhaps borrowing on the silver stockpile. Interest charges and storage charges were completely tax deductible at the time, and it goes without saying that the Hunts are averse to overpaying any income taxes. More politely, one would presume that every legal avenue involving the silver stockpile—hedging in futures markets, and the like—was employed to minimize the tax exposure resulting from the daily river of cash flowing into the Hunt hands from oil, gas, and other income-producing properties, including racehorses.

Today Saudi Arabia has more than $50 billion in official reserves. As a nation holding one of the largest positions in the $800 billion (U.S.) floating outside the United States, it might be expected that Saudi Arabia would do all it could to support and strengthen the dollar abroad. Instead, the thrust of the main dollar holders inside that country is basically to reinvest those dollars in natural assets to replace the oil they produce and sell each day. Their hope is to keep pace with world inflation, which they themselves have helped to create by continually raising the price of oil.

The affairs of the Saudi royal family have always been cloaked in secrecy because of the adverse publicity about family members with a fondness for gambling sorties in Monte Carlo and other casinos. Chances are the Saudis do not seek quick trading profits in their commodity dealings, but rather are content, like Bunker Hunt and his family, to risk dollars in a commodity that will some day emanate the security and profits to justify the risk.

In this connection, a Bermuda corporation, International Metals Investment Company (IMIC), came to life in 1979. Bunker and Herbert Hunt owned one share each, and the remaining shares were divided between two Saudis (Sheik Ali Bin Mussalem and Sheik Mohammed Aboud Al Moudi) and an outfit called Profit Investment Company, Inc. Both Bunker and Herbert Hunt owned interests in Profit Investment, and Herbert helped make trading decisions for the IMIC to acquire physical silver by going long futures, holding until the spot month—then accepting delivery.

Traditionally, 97 to 99 percent of all the open interest on futures exchanges have been settled before the end of the spot month (delivery month) by offset. But the motive for setting up this corporation and its objectives in operating by buying futures and standing for delivery are quite clear. The owners of IMIC wanted physical silver. What better way was there than this to make sure buyers receive triple nine silver in properly hallmarked bars, logged and weighed and numbered? In short, by buying futures and standing for delivery the longs were certain of obtaining fine silver that met Comex and CBOT qualifications.

But by the end of September 1979 it became clear that some of the trade shorts would be unable to deliver Comex grade silver.

There is an old Wall Street adage that goes, "He who sells what isn't his'n must pay the price or go to prison."

Evidently somebody in the futures business was selling something that "isn't his'n," because by the end of September IMIC had accepted delivery of 5,920,000 ounces of Comex September silver, and in October 6,720,000 ounces of CBOT silver. Also in October, IMIC acquired 23 million ounces of silver on an exchange of futures for cash (EFP) with Mocatta. Peculiarly enough, none of this silver was either Comex or CBOT grade. The transaction involved European bullion, silver coins, and forward contracts to be delivered at a later date. At about the same time, IMIC made another EFP with Sharps, Pixley for 4 million silver ounces, not involving American exchange stocks.

One can examine a doughnut and describe it by the outside perimeter or by the inside hole. The implications of these EFPs were cheerily shrugged off by Dr. Jarecki of Mocatta and Mr. Hoffstatter of Sharps, Pixley. But certainly, to professional observers, if Bunker Hunt intended a silver squeeze, why did he enter into EFPs?

In these transactions the number of long contracts held by IMIC were reduced and the number of short contracts held by Mocatta and Sharps were concomitantly reduced. What would have happened if the Hunts and IMIC had demanded triple nine Comex-grade silver?

It is interesting to note that the report of the EFP with Mocatta was passed along to the CFTC by Mocatta. The usual custom is that EFPs appear on the Comex daily sheets, with copies sent to the Commission.

But now that the CFTC plunged into the silver surveillance scene, life became a mad whirl for the Hunt brothers. On October 22 Bunker and Herbert were in Chicago in the offices of the CBOT president. Through the Hunts IMIC had just let the CBOT chairman off the hook by accepting an EFP of 1,344 contracts with him. The following day Bunker went to Washington to discuss silver matters with Read Dunn, commissioner of the CFTC.

At that meeting Bunker made clear that he and his brother were reporting their positions accurately to the CFTC, that they held vault silver (Comex and CBOT stocks) acquired at the time Mocatta made delivery in 1974, and that they had no intention of ever selling that silver or the silver recently acquired. Amazingly enough, Bunker asserted he would exchange triple nine silver held in the vaults for noncertifiable silver either here or in Europe.

In the light of such candor and such gentle and considerate treatment of the shorts, it is almost incredible to learn of the continued cries inside the Comex board of a coming squeeze or "congestion" in any of the future delivery months. But, as we know, the cries grew louder.

Assuredly the action of the Hunts could not be construed as an intention to create a corner in silver. But the CFTC and the exchanges continued to make almost daily surveillance on their positions and those overtly related to their objectives and interests.

The media had made much ado about the personal habits of Bunker Hunt, casting him as a John Belushi character, who gobbles ice cream at a desk, rides in the coach section of airplanes, and wears brown rumpled suits. The media also presents him as a sort of patsy who can be beaten by shrewd traders and con men. No way. Those who know Bunker Hunt know also that he has a keen memory, a shrewd business mind, like a computer, and is a smart, admirable person, with a great gift of rhetoric.

He and Herbert had plenty of cause for complaint when the exchange boards changed the ball game so that the rules could favor one section of the membership who customarily go short on precious metals.

But it certainly seemed puzzling to many market-watchers that the Hunts didn't close the trap on the exposed shorts and break them. Obviously the reason was the existing penalty for market manipulation written into the law covering the CFTC: $100,000 fine and five years in the clink. Surrounded daily by lawyers, the Hunts religiously have avoided becoming embroiled in criminal matters.

They had a run-in some years ago with the government about soybean futures trading allegedly in excess of proscribed limits, and they had to go to court. Chances are they hoped to avoid any adverse publicity that might have arisen had they insisted on taking delivery of their open silver futures when the spot month arrived.

Would H. L. have acted the way his heirs conducted themselves during the silver situation and after? A case could be made either way. The fact is that the Hunts were victimized almost willingly by the predators of the precious metal pits as they shifted their positions from futures contracts in America to physicals at home and abroad.

Do the Hunts have grounds for lawsuits against the involved exchange directors, or perhaps against the exchanges themselves? The lawyers ought to be mighty busy during the coming years.

Obviously the Hunts will have to earn the cash to pay the interest on their $1.1 billion loan. This probably comes to a tax deductible expense of about $200 million a year for the next ten years. Still, if they keep the loan outstanding for the entire length of time, it can readily be imagined what the billion-dollar principal will be worth a decade from the time the loan was effected if inflation continues in the next ten years at the rate we have encountered in the last four.

Many people believe the Hunts have played a rather shrewd numbers game by liquidating their futures during the first three months of 1980 at massive long-term gains and stoically accepting short-term tax losses on the physicals dumped by Bache and others during March 1980. But this is a matter for accountants and perhaps for the Internal Revenue Service. It should be noted that when Bunker met with commissioner Read Dunn in Washington on October 23, he asserted that while he would roll over his existing futures contracts as has been the Hunt practice in the past years, for tax considerations he did not intend to roll over his March position until after January 1, 1980.

Not so oddly, Bunker had a certain level of silver inventory for years in the form of futures. After announcing in January 1980 that he would shift his trading elsewhere, he managed to wind up with a lot more silver in the spring of 1980 than at the beginning of 1979.

How much silver do Bunker and his brother and their allied interests hold and control today? "If you can count it," he claims, "it can't be very much." Will they ever sell it? Possibly their heirs might some day, but not in the foreseeable future.

Chances are there is a lot of H. L. in Bunker, Herbert, Lamar, and the others, including the ladies, their sisters. Having seen silver soar and fall, they all feel it will rise like a phoenix from the ashes as the demand for metal goes up each year. And each year the Hunt private stockpile will probably grow as the cash flows in from the oil and the horses. Better believe the silvered Hunts will remain that way.

Bunker still believes the gold/silver ratio will some day drop to 5 to 1. That is, he believes the time will not be distant when only five ounces of silver will buy one ounce of gold. With gold at $625, that would bring silver to $105 an ounce. At this writing silver is about $16, and the ratio stands at 39/1. Incredible prediction?

In January the ratio ran down at one time to close to the 15/1 level. So Hunt might not be too far off the mark if the exchanges, by their rules, create a market neutral atmosphere between buyers and sellers.

The Hunts, of course, are not alone in their unflagging belief that silver will rise again to levels almost undreamed of. What happened to the other silver bulls? It is fitting to examine how they fared during the roller coaster ride from August 21, 1979, through March 28, 1980, the day after Silver Thursday.

*

EIGHT

*

THE
SILVER
BULLS

In the middle 1950s Norton Waltuch emerged with a degree from Fairleigh Dickinson University in New Jersey and entered the world of business in the export/import area. While living in an apartment house in Fort Lee, N.J., he encountered a neighbor who was a potato trader working the floor of the New York Mercantile Exchange.

"Give me a thousand dollars," pleaded the potato trader, "and I'll make you rich."

Waltuch is not a ruminator. He makes decisions so quickly someone who doesn't know him might think he is reckless. But he thinks quickly and accurately on and off his feet, and he put up the grand.

A week or so later the trader came back to Norton with $10,000. "My God," mused Norton, "where has this been all my life?" From that moment on he became utterly absorbed in the futures markets. Wisely, though, instead of simply plunging with his own capital, he decided to learn from the ground up what causes futures prices to go up and down.

He joined Bache and Company as a trainee and had the opportunity to learn plenty from the experienced people around him, including Charley Mattey and Gerry Gold, author of *Modern Commodities Futures Trading.*

Some time later, when Gold shifted to Hayden-Stone, Waltuch went along as a producer (account executive). By 1970 he had acquired a substantial following of speculative and commercial accounts.

But the firm seemed to be suffering from capital problems, and Waltuch began to worry about the safety of his customers' equities. Quietly, a deal was made between Norton and a newly formed commodity futures trading division of the Continental Grain Company.

Waltuch, assisted by his father, a retired supermarket owner, and a secretary, opened the first New York office for ContiCommodity Services in December 1970. At thirty-seven Norton Waltuch now managed a growing brokerage office, was entrusted with seats on behalf of Continental Grain on all the New York commodity exchanges, and started on the road to riches, his earnings as a manager supplemented by profits in his own trading account.

During most of the decade from 1970 to 1980 Waltuch lived conservatively in suburban New Jersey with his wife and their two children, a son who is sixteen as this is written, and a daughter, thirteen. Norton permitted himself a few personal luxuries, including a condo ski house and a Jaguar.

For most of those years the identity of the customers of Norton Waltuch, like those of Conti and the Grain Company, were kept confidential. And certainly what they were buying or selling, or for whom, had to be as secret as the plans for the newest American missile.

But in 1979, when Norton Waltuch had been elevated into ContiCapital to devote his time only to managing money rather than a branch office with its sea on paperwork and personnel problems, he had to emerge from the secrecy umbrella. Once interviews began with Hy Maidenberg's *New York Times* article on silver in January 1979, the publicity began to make him a public figure, at least in the futures industry. More to the point, it caught the eye of potential customers.

In March 1979 Waltuch acquired an instant reputation as the trader for "Arab interests," or "Middle Eastern interests." This distinction, of course, carried the implication that he enjoyed access to a bottomless pocketbook of Petrodollars, further building his reputation as a power in the market. The funds under ContiCapital's management grew quickly to well over the $100 million mark, and because of the rise in silver at one time they approached $1 billion in equity.

Because of his connection with Conti and Continental Grain, Waltuch's assessment of the markets carried weight that forecasters with lesser connections might have envied. When he forecast a rising trend for silver, he was believed and quickly followed in the market. His bullish silver posture influenced not only managers and account executives of ContiCommodity, but those of friendly and competing firms as well, not to mention Waltuch's customers.

During 1979, when the price of silver almost quintupled from the $5.50 level at the start of the year, Waltuch loomed large across the country and even overseas as a genius whose very presence on the trading floor could cause the price of silver to leap, even when he was not actually buying.

But despite his burgeoning reputation for being "silver-smart," Waltuch had to comply with the wishes of his superior, Walter Goldschmidt. From September 1979 on he reduced the positions in the December and March silver contracts by rolling them forward, liquidating them, or taking delivery.

Moreover, Waltuch knew in January 1980 that, because the trade shorts were imperiled, the Comex board could devise restrictive position limits and possibly adopt liquidation-only rules in order to compel him and his customers, let alone the Hunts, to let go of their holdings in futures contracts.

Since Waltuch is a nonpareil problem solver when it comes to futures trading, he did several things at once.

First, he bought a LeCar to cut down on the gasoline bills for his Jaguar, and began to commute by LeCar.

Second, he advised his customers of the possibility of new and restrictive regulations, and urged them to reduce their positions.

Third, he looked after his own trading account to make sure that he emerged from the coming silver scandal with a profit.

By the end of March 1980 it was reported that Waltuch had grossed up to $20 million in profits. Customers and friends who had hung in and refused to dump their long positions found themselves with little or no profits, or with devastating losses.

The principle that Waltuch understood and acted upon is that in a high-risk operation such as buying and selling silver futures, a trader should select and observe an objective, a preset point at which to exit the market. Those who followed Waltuch at the early stages came out well. Others followed the higher fool theory (you buy something when it has made a new high and hope to sell it at an even higher price) and found themselves faced with disaster.

Other accounts of Waltuch had pursued a different goal: They had never intended to sell, but instead were using the futures market as a means to acquire triple nine silver. These customers found themselves in massive deficit when the remaining futures in their accounts were liquidated and they did not put up the resulting deficit in cash into the clearing firms handling their accounts.

In a *Fortune* article (July 28, 1980) an unnamed associate of Waltuch charges, "He betrayed us." Whether he did or not remains to be seen.

One thing is certain. Waltuch wound up with millions. He became a racehorse owner like the Hunts and Naji Nahas, began to shop around for a large cruiser, sent his daughter off to camp in the summer of 1980, got his son a job on the Comex floor as a messenger, and took his wife Anita away to Italy for a long vacation.

One outcome of his silver success was that Norton Waltuch became a major contributor to many charities, including the United Jewish Appeal and his local Jewish community.

Will Waltuch survive at Conti? Many of his associates and friends in the industry have their doubts. It is not a life-and-death matter to him. He can sell his story, *How I Made $20 Million in Silver,* for big money to an aggressive publisher. A movie could be made around the exciting life he led as he strode into the pits, flew to Europe, wheeled and dealed to raise money for trading.

One of the problems surrounding Waltuch's future relations with Conti involved the deficit created in the account of his largest customer: the silver bull from Sao Paolo, Naji Nahas.

In his early thirties, Nahas is a millionaire many times over. Perhaps he, like Norton Waltuch, may some day make millions by selling his story. How a Lebanese businessman in his thirties directs the fortunes of more than twenty corporations from his base in Sao Paolo, while spending a lot of time in Geneva and Riyadh, ought to make fascinating reading for fans of Horatio Alger success stories.

But since this book is primarily concerned with the silver situation, it is fitting to touch upon how Naji Nahas came to meet and become a client of Norton Waltuch at Conti.

In the past few years Brazil's agriculture has burgeoned far beyond the production of coffee. Brazil's Temperao region has emerged as one of the world's largest producers of cocoa. In the same way, Brazil has become a highly significant producer of oranges and therefore a leading force in the world of frozen orange juice.

Nahas has the burdensome problem of investing a con-

stant cash flow, some of it his, much of it from other investors, some of them Brazilians with a special interest in orange
juice. So it was natural for Nahas to approach Norton Waltuch, who by his own admission is a leading authority on
orange juice, and especially frozen orange juice futures.
Waltuch soon convinced Nahas that there was more money
to be made in silver.

Nahas knew the Hunts, traded in horses like the Hunts,
and knew of their proclivity to acquire, amass, and hold onto
millions of ounces of silver as inflation protection. He went
along with Waltuch's recommendation, and opened a half-
million-dollar account to buy silver futures.

But it developed that Nahas's intentions were not neces-
sarily to follow the dictum of Baron Rothschild to trade in
animals by "buying sheep and trading deer." Instead, Nahas
became convinced, like the Hunts, that silver offered the
only sensible way to protect himself against the declining
value of dollars coming into his various corporations and
won by his horses on the world's race tracks.

On December 18 Naji suffered the indignity of being summoned to appear at 8:30 in the morning before the Comex
special silver committee to explain why he had gone into
silver, how he intended to use silver as a hedge against inflation and as protection against the uncertainties of foreign
currency fluctuations.

Nahas was not a passive witness. He voiced concern at the
margin rules laid down by Comex to stifle investments in
silver. But he insisted he was willing to go along with Comex
to prevent any squeeze on the shorts; he would reduce his
positions in line with the plan already presented to the committee by Walter Goldschmidt of Conti. He also blithely assured the committee that he had no joint ventures with the
Hunt family in silver, but was acting for himself.

Unlike many of the other Conti accounts handled by Waltuch, the Nahas account was not discretionary. That is, Waltuch may have advised him or counseled him on buying and
selling, but the orders and trading decisions were strictly

those of Naji Nahas and whomever he happened to be acting for.

Thus, when the market began to decline at the end of January and during February 1980, Nahas did not roll over or significantly reduce the open contracts in his accounts. Actually, in some instances he added contracts to lower his average cost. So when the collapse occurred on Silver Thursday, his open positions were vastly undermargined by silver's sudden drop of $4 an ounce.

Conti made several attempts to collect the margins from Nahas, but those attempts failed, and this silver bull was involuntarily liquidated, leaving a deficit in his accounts of about $51 million.

Nahas has retained Phil Bloom, a Chicago lawyer, to bring legal action against someone to get back the $51 million, or a good part of it. He will doubtless maintain that he was injured by the self-serving Silver Rule 7 adopted by the Comex board. But none of that solved the $51 million deficit that Nahas owed Conti.

Nahas handed over to Conti $30 million in cash and kind, including steamships, but the remaining $21 million became a write-off in Conti's fiscal year ending March 31, 1980. Conti had a fantastic year for commission earnings, but still nobody likes to lose $21 million.

Did this experience dampen Nahas's enthusiasm for silver? Not one whit. He is a silver bull, and remains bullish. He also owns about 5 million ounces of triple nine silver stored in Comex warehouses, assets that Conti can go after some day if Nahas doesn't pay.

One might wonder why Nahas was treated so leniently by Conti in the light of his deficit. The answer is probably that he did good business with the firm and will probably continue to do business again when his liquidity problems are settled. After all, Federal Reserve chairman Volcker did *not* okay a loan for Nahas as he did for the Hunts. Volcker may have been under the delusion that Nahas acted solely for himself instead of for the Saudis.

It is my arbitrary opinion that the reason Conti has not been harsh with Nahas involves his referrals.

Mahmoud Fustok, at the urging of Naji Nahas, became a customer of Norton Waltuch, and, of course, Conti. Because of his close connections with the Saudi royal family, Fustok, also in his thirties, has become a millionaire many times over. Most of his money came from profits in Saudi real estate, and in such an absolute monarchy it would be difficult to make these millions without the proper regal connections. Fustok's connections with the royal family are so impeccable that, though born a Lebanese, he became a naturalized Saudi. To say that Fustok and his fellow Lebanese, Nahas, worked smoothly as agents for Arab syndicates and members of the Saudi royal family would be to put it mildly.

Unlike Waltuch, Fustok and Nahas were interested in silver futures only as a means of obtaining fine silver and were not interested in profiting by price change. In a word, then, they were investors rather than speculators. And Fustok, unlike Nahas, seemed to have an unlimited reservoir of ready cash.

Assuredly, Fustok's venture into the silver futures market through an American broker was initiated because he mistakenly thought his affairs would be kept confidential and the identity of his account kept secret. He did not reckon with either the inflammatory determination of the CFTC to expose the foreign silver longs or the drive in the Comex board to destroy the confidentiality of clearing member accounts.

Fustok decided to stand for delivery of the silver represented by his long contracts and to avoid being destroyed by the sudden dumping of silver that took place during the last week in March. He continues to take in and pay for the silver in his contracts as the metal is tendered; the chances are that this silver will be buried in the vaults until the end of time.

Where does Fustok get all that cash to pay for the silver?

Frankly, that is his business, but obviously the cash flow from both oil and Saudi real estate keeps climbing. Come to think of it, if you ever get a chance to walk through the winding alleys that snake through London back of Fleet Street, you will come upon building after building bearing signs in Arabic and English indicating the Saudi presence in that city. And from the events that have occurred in the silver market during 1979 and 1980, it is a foregone conclusion that the silver exchanges in the United States will have to live with the overhang of the Hunt physicals lying in the vaults as well as with the millions of ounces held by Mahmoud Fustok, who doesn't like to lose money.

One of Norton Waltuch's associates in ContiCapital was Tom Waldeck. In his early forties, Waldeck is a dignified, intelligent grain trader, who worked for Continental Grain in Geneva before joining Ivan Auer and Norton Waltuch to form the key management triumvirate of ContiCapital.

Tom Waldeck, of course, was well acquainted in Geneva banking circles. When interest in silver began to rise in 1979, it was natural for the Swiss bankers who knew him to come to Waldeck and Conti to handle their trading on the American exchanges. Banque Populaire's pooled account swelled to include forty-five so-called "foreign" investors with impressive resources; the identity of the principals is still a secret despite the ongoing efforts of CFTC. The clients at Banque Populaire Suisse (Volksbank) were mainly accounts of Advicorp, a Swiss investment advisory service.

As the price of silver began its gradual descent into the depths from the Matterhorn-like top of $50 in January, some of the Volksbank clients rolled over or took delivery rather than liquidate. On balance, it is presumed there were more losers than winners in these accounts, since speculators have a well-known tendency to hang on to whatever they own while the price collapses rather than sell in good time. Always they hope for a price rebound and recovery.

Moreover, like Nahas and other silver bulls who were destroyed by the shorts, the Swiss accounts might well recover much of their losses through legal action in the future.

To say the least, the silver market of 1979–80 and the actions of the CBOT and Comex boards will provide an ongoing feast for lawyers all over the world. Despite the alleged fears of the exchange boards, there was never any real danger of a squeeze on the shorts or a corner in silver. However unreal the basis was for those fears, the losses suffered by the market participants were quite real, and that is the stuff of lawsuits.

How much money Tom Waldeck made or lost on the silver market is, of course, his business. And the extent of Norton Waltuch's profits would be purely a private matter if he had not given *Fortune* a more modest number. But it is certainly evident that Waltuch and Waldeck, or both, can go their own way any time they please to manage money for people who want to assume the risks of the futures markets. They can do this with or without Conti.

Phil Lindstrom is sixty-two and has slaved thirty-eight years for Hecla Mining Company. At this writing he is the employee with the longest span of service at that company, and possibly he will get a gold—or, better, a silver—watch one day if he ever chooses to retire. That day may come sooner than Lindstrom cares to think, because something terrible happened to him as the price of silver began to soar in 1979.

Phil Lindstrom remembers well the plodding years of the silver business, when, under the Silver Act of 1934, the mining companies were compelled to sell all their silver to the U.S. government at 64.64 cents an ounce. Imagine how his heart leaped when he watched the price go from $5.50 to over $9 in August 1979, and then in October when the price moved more in one day than it had in fourteen years, from 1950 to 1964.

This proved too much for Phil. He suffered a myocardial arrest.

Lying in the hospital, he watched the silver price soar to $25 and then, as he went into convalescence, to $50 an ounce. He also watched the shares of stock in the mining company he works for, Hecla Mining, rise from 4⅝ in December 1978 to $53 in January 1980.

Lindstrom, who probably knows more about the fundamentals involving silver than any other man alive, recovered completely by the time the price dropped on Silver Thursday to $10.80. He is back on the trail again to help investment analysts all over the world appreciate the inherent value of Hecla stock.

How did he fare in the price collapse? In a modest manner he confesses, "I bought a little more silver. The world's running out of silver, you know—and I can't think of a better investment."

In November 1979 Jim Blanchard conducted probably the largest precious metals conference ever envisioned by man. More than 3,200 attendees assembled the first week of November 1979 at the Hyatt Regency Hotel in New Orleans paying about $400 each to listen to speakers from all over the world and to attend workshops on such specialized matters as tax shelters and Swiss bank accounts.

But this tremendously successful "goldbug" conference did not happen by accident. It happened because of Jim Blanchard, a leading silver bull.

Blanchard is a self-made multimillionaire, who parlayed his university-born interest in free market economics and a keen sense of timing into growing and diverse business enterprises, including precious metals investments, foreign and U.S. real estate, publishing, investment conferences, and his own company specializing in coins, precious metals, and other inflation hedges, including fine art.

A relatively young man for such a stunning business success, Jim's achievements become even more remarkable when one learns he has accomplished all this from a wheelchair. He is paralyzed from the waist down. Despite this, he conducts investment conferences in all parts of the world, from New Orleans to Montreal to Acapulco to Hong Kong.

Jim is a firm believer in silver. It did not surprise him greatly when the white metal rose to $50, nor did he become distressed when it collapsed to below $11 in March 1980.

Like Lindstrom, the Idaho silver bull, and Fustok, the Saudi silver bull, Blanchard increases his pile of silver and silver coins every year—and hopes never to sell, no matter what price silver ever reaches. If the ascent from $5.50 to $50 seemed like climbing the Matterhorn, Jim feels a climb to Everest is in the offing after the Hunt situation is finally settled.

Meantime, he issues his *Gold Letter* and his *Market Alert,* making the case that, despite temporary setbacks, the 1980s will be the decade of tangibles, with huge amounts of investment and institutional capital flowing into precious metals.

Many of the silver bulls are in their early thirties, and Jim Blakely is no exception. He lives on a hillside near Newtown, Connecticut, with his wife and two children (a boy of seven and a girl of five). In 1976 Jim founded the *Silver and Gold Report* and became one of the most successful market-letter editors in the country. His one complaint since then is that references to his *Silver and Gold Report* are generally distorted by the media into *Gold and Silver Report* because editors like to put first things first—and alphabetically.

But to Jim Blakely silver has always come before gold. Even in the gold/silver ratio, he claims, silver comes first. Having made a substantial profit himself in the silver futures market, where did he stand when the collapse came to the silver price in March 1980?

"I, like Hunt," he said, "got out of futures and into physical silver and coins. Frankly, I am becoming more and more interested in silver coins, because their downside potential is a lot less than the downside risks in silver or silver futures."

His eyes twinkle merrily behind silver-rimmed glasses as he picks up copy for the next issue of his *Silver and Gold Report* and asks, "Sarnoff, do you think the futures markets will ever come back in silver?"

This is a question the silver longs who got bloodied in March 1980 are asking themselves. The question also troubles the commodity futures brokers, who earn their sustenance from earned trading commissions and are painfully aware that for the first three months of 1980 silver trading volume stood at only 10 percent of the level of a year earlier. Then the silver futures markets were low-margined, high-leveraged arenas where a trader could prosper by selling on strength and buying on weakness, or buying on weakness and selling on strength.

Recently Comex has reduced initial margin for speculators to $5,000 a contract from a high of $75,000 earlier in 1980. But alas, the Comex and CBOT boards have made the rules so restrictive that only small players can be attracted to the silver game. A margin of $5,000 is still rather high for a contract covering only $80,000 worth of silver. Still, optimism never dies in the hearts of marketing VPs, including those who slave for commodity exchanges.

The marketing experts at CBOT have made a plea to the CFTC to permit the exchange to reduce the size of the contract from 5,000 ounces to 1,000 ounces. If this were done, would margins be split also, to $1,000?

One thing is certain: Even if the margins were reduced by 80 percent, the commissions would not be reduced by that amount. But if the silver exchanges again attract speculator interest to the extent that the silver bulls rise from the dust, what chance will these silver bulls have of making a killing?

In his treatise on how to squeeze the silver market, Henry

Jarecki maintained that a number of people in the past have tried to buy enough silver to affect prices. He further claims they have failed to do so because they have been trapped by:

1. An underestimation of the money needed to achieve success and to meet margin calls.
2. The costs of interest in carrying physicals.
3. Increasing faith in their own market wisdom.
4. Failure to understand that not everybody can leave by the same door.

The doctor failed to mention that well-heeled speculators may also fail if the rules of the game are suddenly changed by the set of players who seem to be losing the game.

Though this book is entitled *Silver Bulls,* it would not be fair to end our assessment of the "silver situation" without mentioning how the major Comex shorts fared during the silver price collapse from the third week in January to the end of March 1980.

Mocatta Metals, according to its chairman, enjoyed a record first quarter in 1980 and wound up, in his opinion, as the second largest privately owned firm in America. Philipp Brothers Division of Engelhard Metals made a significant contribution to its parent from trading profits during the first three months of 1980. The parent company claims the $400 million item involving the Hunt contract cancellation of a silver purchase at $35 an ounce had "zero effect" on the company earnings.

And what happened to the hapless Alfredo Fonseca?

According to former fellow employees in Lima, Peru, "he has disappeared." So, evidently, has MINPECO's $80 million, at least temporarily. In the light of what happened, assuredly some shrewd lawyer may convince MINPECO it has sound grounds for recovery.

As to the affairs of J. Aron, represented on the Comex

board by H. Coyne, and of Sharps, Pixley, represented on the same exchange board by Mr. Hoffstatter, Jr., it is practically a certainty that they laughed all the way down to the bank.

Thus ends the Sarnoff version of what happened during the time the exchanges now called "the silver situation." Voltaire once said: "The secret of being a bore is to tell everything." What has been omitted will probably emerge some day in pretrial examinations, as lawyers for the longs who lost billions in the silver collapse sue to recover. Very possibly, lawyers for the shorts who were taken to the cleaners on the silver rise may also sue. They may well contend that they were the victims of the trade shorts who sit on the exchange boards and, as market operators, were constantly hiking the price.

Who will win is anybody's guess. Suffice to say there are a lot of nervous people commuting daily to work in the futures industry. Probably they are waiting to see what the lawyers will do.

Meanwhile, it may make sense to discuss some basic silver trading strategies.

*

NINE

*

SILVER TRADING STRATEGIES

Gold and silver, like coffee and cream, have gone together in the minds of the poor and the rich since biblical times. Indeed, in ancient times the hard money of most countries involved gold for the expensive coins and silver for the inexpensive coinage. Last year, incredibly, ninety-nine countries struck silver coins, while in America silver coinage came virtually to a halt after 1964.

But back in 1896, when the United States had a bimetallic monetary system using both silver and gold, the gold/silver ratio stood at 16 to 1. That is, officially it took sixteen ounces of silver to equal the value of one ounce of gold. In the free world market at that time the ratio proved to be closer to 32 to 1. This caused Chauncey DePew, for fifty years leader of the New York Central Railroad, to thunder: "Where is the sacredness that makes sixteen ounces of silver for one ounce of gold the foundation stone of our national greatness, business prosperity, and human happiness?"

DePew's agitation at that time becomes understandable because he referred to a gold/silver ratio made by law instead of by the forces in the marketplace. Today, of course, the monetary system in the United States has neither gold nor silver behind the paper currency in circulation. All we have, sadly, is a hard-working printing press and coins of base metals.

Most readers may know of, or recall, the confiscation of American gold by the government in 1933 to "strengthen" our currency. But perhaps few of our readers realize that the following year, 1934, the government passed the Silver Act, confiscating the silver in the hands of citizens at 50 cents an ounce, though silver coins were permitted to remain in circulation. Thereupon the United States government acquired a vast inventory of silver, approximating 2 billion ounces.

Because of consistent and continuous efforts by the Silver Users Association and other lobbying groups, the government has managed to dispose of all but 139.5 million ounces from the stockpile, mainly at $1.29 an ounce. When silver hit $50 an ounce, the value of the remaining silver in the national stockpile approximated $7 billion. But efforts of the lobbyists to sell the silver failed in 1979, as they will fail in 1980, because the government ought to buy, not sell, silver.

Silver, the second most popular precious metal, occurs mainly uncombined in nature. In addition to ores that are primarily composed of silver, however, the white metal is also found in nature associated with copper, lead, and other metals as a secondary ore product. In 1979 the Soviet Union overtook Mexico as the world's largest silver producer, the result of its having stepped up its stockpiling goals for all strategic metals. Probably Mexico will return next year as the leading silver supplier to the world—with Peru and the United States and Canada producing almost equal amounts, making second, third, and fourth places inconsequential.

Normally, silver is refined and cast into bars of approximately 1,000 ounces with 99.9 percent purity. Before the London Metal Exchange opened in 1877, silver, like other metals, traded on a cash basis. Users could contract to take a supply of silver from mining companies or bullion dealers to be delivered on certain forward dates, but in essence markets were cash delivery. Title to the metal, rather than contracts to buy or to deliver, changed hands.

Today a risk-taker can seek profits from price changes in silver in many forms. But the most popular forms of participation are as follows:

1. Silver physicals
2. Silver Coin Bags
3. Silver Coins (Rare)
4. Silver forward or futures contracts
5. Silver Options
6. Silver Leverage Contracts
7. Silver Shares
8. Silver Spreads

Obviously, the risk-taker in silver has a plethora of choices for investment or speculative purposes, with the degree of risk varying according to (a) the leverage involved; and (b) the volatility of the category selected. For example, at one time it took only $1,000 in margin to buy a contract on 5,000 ounces of silver. Thus if silver dropped 20 cents an ounce, the holder's margin would be wiped out. On the other hand, if the holder had purchased and paid for a 1,000-ounce bar of silver at, say, $5 an ounce, he would have had zero leverage, but would not have been wiped out if the silver had dropped to $4.80.

Each of the silver-related forms of risk-taking has its history. Each has its legitimate uses for investment or speculation. With one exception. That is the silver leverage contract. That form was invented by boiler room artists for the purpose of separating the gullible from their money, and in my judgment it should be rigidly avoided by everybody.

Outside that single exception there is growing merit in using any of the other media for silver trading, although some may have more drawbacks than others.

1. SILVER PHYSICALS

Although the standard triple nine silver bar that represents good delivery on Comex, CBOT, and LME comes in bars approximating 1,000 ounces, silver bullion may be obtained in as small a quantity as a single ounce. The Swiss Bank, Deak Penera, Manfred Tortella & Brooks, and other dealers offer silver "ingots" (actually stampings) as small as one ounce.

Premiums are generally charged by the seller for silver bullion delivered in lots of less than 10,000 ounces. For example, the purchaser of a 1,000-ounce bar will pay a premium of anywhere from 3 to 8 percent above the spot price fixed in London on the day of the sale, while the buyer of a 1-ounce silver sliver from the Swiss Bank may pay as much as 25 to 35 percent premium over the fix because of the small quantity involved and the cost of the paperwork to log the sale.

If silver bars are purchased for all cash, and delivery is taken, they should be kept in a safe place. A home is not a safe place; and if the owner of bars wants complete safety and security, he or she will have to store the bars at an accredited warehouse or bank, which means paying insurance and storage. Since charges for this service vary, they should be determined well in advance of any purchase. Storage charges and any interest involved—if the bars are hocked—are normally treated as tax deductions from ordinary income. Insurance charges for safekeeping silver bars are not tax deductible. In addition, many states levy a sales and use tax on purchase of physical silver as on gold bullion. That is why many buyers use the futures contract market and take delivery of their silver in warehouses overseas.

The problem that arises from storage of precious metals overseas at a safe depository is that from time to time such supposedly safe countries as Switzerland enact storage taxes, adding to an investor's cost of holding physicals. And, of course, investors who put their after-tax money into silver and send the silver for storage outside the United States may be sending their property to a country that encounters a revolution or switches from capitalism to communism, as in the cases of Cuba and Afghanistan.

The very real problem of selling or liquidating bars of silver may also deter nonprofessionals from sinking a lot of money into silver in this form. If the silver bars are left in a certified safe depository, ownership is reflected by a proper warehouse receipt. Thus, to sell such silver, the owner simply surrenders the warehouse receipt in order to collect the resulting funds. But if the owner of silver bars actually wants to take possession of his silver, he may have it delivered via Brink's to his bank in Podunk. There the proud owner loads the bars in a strong station wagon and hauls them home to a closet in the basement. Fine so far. But when he is ready to sell, the problems arise. Bullion dealers trust everybody, but they always cut the bars. By this we mean that the sale will not be fulfilled until the bars have been weighed and analyzed at the seller's expense.

So a bit of friendly advice is, never take possession of silver bars unless you intend to do one or both of two things: (a) pass the bars along to an heir or other person; and (b) shift part of your estate to some other country by sending the silver bullion abroad.

Silver, like gold, is portable, exportable, and quite often nonreportable, so it, like the Midas metal, lends itself to ready transference of wealth if the transferor wants to undergo the risks of avoiding estate taxes.

A person can walk into the Swiss Bank at the World Trade Center, when silver is, say, $15 for London spot, and buy one-ounce ingots from the bank at $20.50 each plus the 8 percent New York sales tax. The bank does not record the risk-taker's name or social security number. Maybe that is why the bank does such a brisk business in both silver "ingots" and gold coins.

Of course, there is nothing basically wrong with accumulating small amounts of silver over a long period of time on a regular basis. For example, had an investor purchased an ounce of silver at the London fixing every trading day of 1979, his average cost would have been $11.09 plus the premium. At year-end silver stood at over $25, and profits could have been made even after the discount of selling one-ounce quantities.

The basic problem of leveraging silver bullion in bar form is simply the danger of changing interest rates and storage and insurance charges for carrying the bullion. A perfect example of this befell the Hunts when they switched from carrying futures contracts to carrying physical metal at Bache Halsey Stuart Metals. Interest rates went from 15¾ prime in the United States to 20 percent in the space of a few weeks, and though the silver was probably stored by Bache in London, assuredly the loan came from the States at several percentage points above the prime. Those of you who want to do a terrifying mental exercise can multiply 35 million ounces by $16 an ounce and then calculate the daily interest paid on such a loan.

That is why Bunker Hunt's $400 million settlement with Engelhard Minerals (Philipp Brothers) of a contract to purchase silver at $35 an ounce came about with the Hunts gladly paying the differential between $35 and the then market price of about $15 so that they wouldn't have the burden of paying for and carrying the silver. Besides, according to tax authorities, the dissolution of this contract between the Hunts and Engelhard resulted in a massive deduction from ordinary income for the loss.

For those investors who plan to hold on to silver for many years and possibly pass it along to their children, it might make sense to set up a plan to buy one-ounce ingots on a regular basis from such sources as the Swiss Bank. If the investor has sources of capital, as do the Hunts or the Saudi royal family, then an accumulation program that involves leveraging could be useful.

Personally, I have never favored tying up money in physical bullion unless I could put the bullion to work by granting precious metal options. This is a rather difficult strategy to accomplish at the present time because of the CFTC rule banning American FCMs from offering LME options on silver. But hopefully someday this ban may be lifted, and at that time I will probably, if still around, do a book on precious metals option granting strategies.

At this time it is enough to say that by resorting to such a strategy the risk-taker reduces the cost of the inventory used to protect the outstanding silver options and also reduces the interest costs of carrying such inventory. It is interesting to note that while Nahas and the Hunts consistently claim they were not in the silver market "in concert," in March 1980 Nahas seems to have granted silver options to both Bunker and Herbert Hunt. Ah, well. All these gentlemen are intensely interested in racehorses; why shouldn't they make deals in silver, including options?

Interestingly enough, silver has outperformed all the other precious metals pricewise during the past decade. Here is a table indicating some interesting price changes:

Precious Metal	Price: 1970	High: 1980	#Times Multiplied During decade '70–'80
Gold	$40	$875	almost 22
Silver	$1.70	$50	29
Platinum	$80	$1025	almost 13

Even more dramatic are the records of the past indicating that silver has outperformed all other metals since the great American depression of the 1930s. In 1930, a half-century ago, silver went begging at 36 cents an ounce. In early 1980 it reached $49.60 for spot metal. Thus, in the past fifty years the price of the white metal multiplied itself about 138 times, proof that the silver bulls are not completely crazy.

Naturally, it is the nature of silver to undergo volatility at times, offering traders the chance to make money not only on price rises but also on price declines. That is why there has been such keen interest in silver futures by speculators of varying degrees of wealth—interest, that is, until the directors at the exchanges distorted the rules to suit their short positions.

But before enlarging on the trading techniques available in trading futures it is fitting to touch upon another—and perhaps safer—area of owning silver in physical form.

2. SILVER COIN BAGS

From 1896 until the end of 1964 the dollars, halves, quarters, and dimes minted and circulated in the United States by our government contained 90 percent silver. From 1965 on most of the coins struck for circulation as money have had no silver in them. So obviously the circulated coins containing silver should theoretically have become more valuable than their face as the price of silver rose. And valuable indeed they became.

Some enterprising merchants a few years ago decided that silver coin bags of $1,000 face value were a readily marketable item, since futures contracts of ten bags, each containing silver halves, quarters or dimes, were traded on the floor of the New York Mercantile Exchange. There were plenty of coin bags around to make delivery, since the trading interest in the Merc's coin bag contract amounted to peanuts.

So a West Coast dealer, scenting an opportunity for profit, went to work to promote its coin bags through a seminar approach. All the factors for this promotion seemed favorable. The face value of the coins was $1,000, and the bags were trading only a little above face value of the coins. People were invited to free seminars across the country, and the approach at each seminar was the same: "We don't want to sell you anything, we just want you to know (via a movie) that things in the USA will soon be as they were in Germany after World War One, when a person had to wheel a wheelbarrow full of green German marks down to the bakery just to buy bread."

The Pacific Coast Coin Exchange (PCC), which of course was a dealer and not an exchange, had to fight off buyers rushing to the tables where salesmen waited. At the time I remarked to my associate, "All they have to do is be honest and all the money in the banks will eventually wind up in silver bags—if there are that many bags."

Evidently being honest in business is awfully hard if the firm is unethical or greedy. Not content to take silver bags that were trading for, say, $1,250 and selling them at retail for $1,450, this so-called exchange offered a leverage deal to the unwary investor.

If the bag buyer paid in full for one bag, Pacific Coast would buy the account two more bags and charge interest, storage, insurance, etc. Of course, at any time the investor could sell one bag, or two bags, or even all three and end the arrangement; or the bag buyer could sell off one or two bags and take delivery on the third; or he could pay up for all three bags at the original entry price and either store the bags with PCC or take actual delivery via bonded messenger, such as Brink's. Since there are 710 ounces of fine silver in one of these $1,000 bags, an investor could quickly calculate the value of the silver in each bag offered by multiplying the going silver fix by 710. So if silver traded at $2 an ounce, the bag was worth $1,420, and a ten-bag purchase would involve $14,200, while a three-bag, leveraged PCC purchase involved roughly $5,000. After all, PCC had to be repaid for the expense of the seminars that brought the leveraged bag bonanza to the potential customer's attention.

But PCC sold so many bags to so many people that the obvious temptation to go short against the purchases and charge storage, interest, and commissions on property it had not even acquired proved to be irresistible. After purchasers began to complain several years later that they could not get their silver bags, the SEC and the State of California acted to put PCC out of business.

Still, coin bags are an excellent way to play the silver market. One of my friends, who declines to have his name mentioned, once purchased hundreds and hundreds of silver bags when they were almost at face value and hocked them with a friendly bank. Over the years he paid interest of a tax deductible nature and reduced his ordinary income by the amount of the interest so paid. He had made his original purchases by buying coin bag futures on the New York Merc and accepting delivery, paying in full for the bags as the spot month arrived and then taking them to the bank to get a loan of at least $1,000 a bag. The bank, of course, welcomed such a loan, since it took absolutely no risk, holding $1,000 of liquid collateral that couldn't possibly depreciate for every $1,000 advanced to the customer. Indeed, for banks such a loan is a dream.

Despite urging of well-meaning friends and counselors, our hero hung on to his bags, paying interest through the nose as rates rose over the years and getting in turn larger deductions from ordinary income. But then came 1979. With silver at $20 an ounce, each ten-bag lot now appeared to be worth $142,000 vs. an average cost of $12,000 a lot, or $1,200 a bag.

Did he sell?

December 1979 passed, and he did nothing. But when the silver price soared to $40 in the early part of January he could no longer wait. At about $40 he unloaded his bags. Profits, of course, ran into the millions, all of it long-term gain. Maybe Bunker knew something when he effected the EFPs with Mocatta, Sharps, Pixley, and J. Aron in October 1979 involving substitution of coin bags for triple nine silver.

Having unloaded his bags at an average price of over a quarter of a million dollars for each ten-bag lot, which had cost him only $12,000 a decade ago, what did our hero do?

The day after Silver Thursday he appeared out of the blue

at my office. I hadn't seen him for some years. "You still have your bags?" I asked politely.

He looked nervously down at the floor and mumbled: "I sold them too soon, when silver was around $40." Then, before I even made any comment, he said, "But I can't live without silver bags, so I bought a lot of them back yesterday." 'Yesterday' silver stood at $11 in London. By the time he told me about his adventure with silver bags it was $13. Probably he'll replace most of the bags sold at the $40 silver level, take them to the bank when delivery month arrives, and start all over. Only this time his risk is cushioned by a multimillion-dollar, long-term capital gain.

The silver bag futures are traded on the New York Mercantile Exchange each trading day in a very thin market. Substantial purchase or sales orders affect price radically, so an assessment of future timing and market atmosphere is critical for any trader. Anyone intending to take delivery and hold the bags for eternity can purchase them any time. No silver-content, pre-1965 American coins will ever be minted again, so there is a modicum of collector sentiment in the coins themselves.

The bags do not contain bright uncirculated silver coins. The coins are circulated and in quality may range from very good to simply poor. For some years before the silver market explosion of 1979-80 silver bags futures traded at a discount to the actual price of silver futures contracts on CBOT and Comex. But that condition has practically disappeared.

At one time the New York Merc traded a silver dollar bag contract containing Morgan dollars. But inactivity in this contract caused it to be withdrawn. Oddly enough, though the silver dollars also contain 90 percent silver, they are more prized as collectors items than are smaller silver coins.

3. SILVER COINS (RARE)
During 1979 our benignant government decided to offer at "fair" prices some Carson City silver dollars held in storage

since the nineteenth century. Initially the offering price of a limited amount of these coins was to be in the neighborhood of $30 per coin; this was then hiked to $40 or $45. But by the time the government got around to offering these collector coins the price was $60 to $65.

A limit per purchase per person was put on this offer, and the offering immediately went out the window, as they say in Wall Street. Thousands of investors sent in forms and checks and awaited their silver dollar treasure. But by the time the government got around to mailing the coins and depositing the customers' checks, the price of silver had dropped into the tank. At the time of the offering the silver value inside each coin approximated $40. By the time the coins were shipped, that value had dropped to $16.

Of course, the people got their coins, but the government got screwed in the process. About $7 million in stop payment and bounced checks came back to the agency selling the coins. Experts believe it will cost the government at least $100 to collect each $60 or $65 involved in the useless checks.

Not to be deterred—and to demonstrate that the value of collector coins does not depend significantly on the value of the metal inside the coins—the government, in the summer of 1980, announced another offering of Carson City silver dollars. This time the price is $150. And this time the government insists on exercising its motto on the coinage, "In God We Trust"—only certified bank checks or money orders are acceptable. How much is silver, anyway? It stood at about $16 when this latest silver dollar offering was announced.

Not everyone can afford to buy gold bullion coins or gold collector coins. But silver collector coins are within the reach of almost everyone.

Oddly enough, the most interest lies in silver dollars. In 1979 an 1801 silver dollar sold at auction for $401,000. Even experts had to admit that seemed to be a rather steep price for a silver dollar, higher, in fact, than one of the St. Gaudens $20 gold pieces that did not stack only (six or so in the world) would bring, because that coin went in the vicinity of

$300,000. Lo and behold, during the first half of 1980 the same silver dollar coin found itself resold for a mere $525,000!

Every once in a while large ads appear in the financial pages of leading newspapers offering liquidation of estate-held silver dollars. For some unexplained reason I have always noticed these ads, but have never taken advantage of them. Just recently one advertisement offered 1891-S "rare Morgan silver dollars" in bright, uncirculated rolls of twenty at $5,500 per roll, or $275 per coin. The ad also announced to the world that silver dollars have appreciated over the past decade at the rate of 52 percent per year. If someone would guarantee the continuance of such a pattern, my normally conservative Yankee-Russian background might lead me to dip into my reserves and acquire such growth merchandise.

Coin collectors are helped by the tax laws because they can receive capital gains without paying taxes as long as they upgrade the coins that are replaced after sale. For example, if an investor buys a silver dollar at $100, keeps it for several years, then decides to sell for $200, he or she would have no tax liability on the gain if the proceeds were invested in another coin worth, say, $250. Subsequently, if this coin appreciated to $500 and were sold, no capital gains tax would be charged if the investor bought a coin costing more than the $500 disposal price.

This practice has given rise to an army of experts and coin counselors, who not only help people build portfolios designed to continue appreciating forever, but also do a thriving business between clients who have used their services to put buyer and seller together.

It might make good sense to seek out accredited experts before buying silver dollars, halves, quarters, etc., for collector purposes. Obviously, these markets are cushioned by the constant influx of new collectors and therefore are not normally as volatile as markets involving silver futures or physicals.

The big problem that exists in the collector coin market is liquidity. If a distress sale is required, the investor may find that a coin catalogued at a much higher figure will bring a very low price because the dealer has to put it in inventory and never knows when he or she will be able to sell it at a profit to somebody else. Another problem involving investing in silver coins is simply that the collection—if it is sizable—throws off no dividends or monetary return until it is eventually sold or auctioned.

Still, for those who desire to compress the size of their estate into a small package and are reluctant to buy large, perfect diamonds, silver coins of collector quality may be the answer.

4. SILVER FORWARD OR FUTURES CONTRACTS

Silver forward contracts (metal for three-month delivery) are traded daily in the ring at the London Metal Exchange. A small number of representatives of ring members are seated in a circle and, for the period of each five-minute "ring" in which silver is traded, arrive at a mutually satisfactory ring price upon which buy and sell orders are based until the next trading session. Unlike futures contracts that are customarily settled by offset, LME contracts contemplate actual delivery of the involved metal.

Thus, assume a user desires to purchase one LME forward contract of silver for an agreed price of 700 pence per ounce for delivery precisely three months from the date of this contract unless the maturity date falls on a weekend or a national holiday. The warehouse receipt for this 10,000-ounce silver contract will be delivered to the buyer, and the buyer, of course, will pay for the involved silver. A speculator can go long a three-month silver contract and get out of his obligation at any time up to the delivery or "prompt" date simply by offering 10,000 ounces at the going price for that particular date. If there is a taker to the offer, then the former long has been replaced by a new long and the contract remains in force.

Conversely, if the speculator who didn't have any silver thinks the price is too high and wants to short a contract or two, then his ring member sells the forward metal to another ring member representing a buyer, etc. If the short wants to wipe out his obligation, he simply enters the market through his broker and buys a similar contract for the same prompt date.

Thus, on the LME there can hardly exist under normal trading circumstances conditions such as "congestion" (the major long position in a few hands), since the LME is a delivery market rather than a market where contracts are issued and canceled by offset. On the LME delivery can take place on any business day, and is not limited to fixed delivery dates as in U.S. exchanges. In other words, traders can achieve an average price by participating every day, since silver is bought and sold for forward or future delivery every trading day.

With restrictive margin and position rules that hit American silver markets during October 1979 and January 1980, who can blame the Hunts and other large customers for deserting the New York and Chicago futures exchanges? The LME has no daily trading limits and no position limits. It doesn't care who the buyers and sellers are or how much they buy and sell. The main item that concerns the LME is the ability of its members to live up to the contracts that they make each day. And it doesn't matter to the LME board of governors whether Soviets, Chinese, Peruvians, or Americans are dealing through ring members. Confidentiality of a customer's accounts and positions are held sacred and not blabbed to the press, as was the case when Comex revealed who Conti's large customers were.

One of the directors of Comex collared me at Henry Jarecki's annual pool party in mid-July 1980 and said, "You know, Paul, when a firm has gone on the wrong side of the market and is caught short with silver rising every day, and the firm's capital is going down the drain due to variation margin, and the firm's trader may be getting a heart attack in the process, how can you blame them for doing everything they can to creep out of the trouble?"

My answer was, "They shouldn't have been short in the first place if they didn't have sources of getting the metal to cover."

As previously mentioned, on the Comex and the CBOT, futures contract trades involve 5,000-ounce lots of triple nine silver in 1,000-ounce bars. For every penny of change in the silver price the value of a contract rises or falls fifty dollars. Before August 1979 a limit-move of 20 cents per ounce (change in value of $1,000 a contract) occurred only on rare occasions, but moves of three to five cents during a trading session—up or down or both ways—were not uncommon.

In 1978 initial margins were raised from $1,000 to $2,000. Thus, the minimum price change required to double a margin (or wipe it out) rose to 40 cents. Volatility increased as shorts engulfed the markets seeking ever higher average prices, and the margins were repeatedly raised in order to cause the longs to let go. When it became apparent that the longs were not deterred by higher margins, the shorts devised the position-limit and liquidation-only rules that eventually destroyed the longs as interest rates rose.

After the debacle of Silver Thursday, the Comex and the CBOT sought ways to lure back speculators who may have been ruined by being short on the rise or were devastated by being long on the drop of the silver price.

One of the ways involved lowering of the initial margins and permitting more lenient spread margins. This has been attempted, but the rules have not been eased enough to re-attract the kind of brisk and growing futures trade in silver that both exchanges enjoyed in 1978 and 1979.

Another marketing ploy is the attempt to reduce the size of the contract, since silver is still trading about three times higher than it was in 1978. Will the efforts of the exchanges to woo back the speculating public be successful?

That's their worry, not ours. The commission merchant who deals in futures is always reluctant to suggest his customers take risk in markets that are not market neutral. And so long as the trade influences sway the thinking of the Comex board, the silver market cannot make a comeback, whether the size of the contract is shrunk to 1,000 ounces or remains at 5,000. It can only make a comeback if the rules remain fair to the speculator.

Hardly anyone who goes to a gambling house is averse to losing, provided the gambler feels the games are fair. But he certainly takes umbrage when it is crystal clear that the game has been rigged in favor of the house. Naturally, it is not completely fair to compare a casino with a legitimate trading arena that is supposed to offer opportunity to both hedgers and speculators to participate in futures trading. But serious concerns and doubts are raised when articles such as the one in *Fortune* entitled "Corruption in the Commodity Markets" (July 28) make widespread the mephitic activity of the exchange boards during a period of unusual stress.

In any event, a potential risk-taker in commodity futures contracts involving silver has to open an account with a registered futures commission merchant, sign proper papers, make a proper opening deposit, according to the requirements of the firm (usually $5,000 or $10,000), and agree to maintain the account by inserting financial infusions of variation margins when and if needed. Thereafter the risk-taker has the choice of handling his or her own account, or relying on the trading decisions of an experienced person servicing the account. To arrange a discretionary account, the customer has to sign a limited power of attorney giving the account executive or adviser the right to enter buy or sell orders for the account at the service person's "discretion."

Experience indicates that discretion given is usually money lost. Despite the strident claims of the many money managers who cream off fees from the top of any account given them (usually 15 to 25 percent) normally about 70 percent of the speculators lose money trading futures. Why? Well, even if they handle the account themselves and devote their full time to it, chances are they have not made a proper trading plan, nor modified it in the light of changing markets.

Here is some advice that may help you to trade successfuly in silver futures:

1. If you decide to trade in silver, learn all you can about the fundamental supply/demand situation in the metal. You can obtain free fundamental information from any FCM who is a member of a major exchange and handles public accounts.

2. Watch volume and open interest changes on the exchange you prefer to trade in. Decide on trading either in New York or Chicago or even the LME in London. Select one and confine your activity only to the exchange whose rules you can understand. Copy of the rules may be had from any exchange member, but of course the rules are subject to change.

3. Obtain charts showing action in the price of silver futures for the past six months, and particularly examine charts covering the month you want to trade in.

4. Since the nearest three months are the most popular ones, trade in the one not closest to the spot or delivery month. Avoid transactions in the spot month unless you are three inches from the silver pit. Charts are available, generally free, from any FCM who services customer accounts. And subscriptions can be entered for futures charts. One of the best sources is Commodity Research Bureau, One Liberty Plaza, New York City; another is Commodity Concepts, Chicago. Best source for LME silver charts is Investment Research, Panton Street, Cambridge, England.

5. Decide on a plan of action after reading some basic commodity books like Mark Powers, *Getting Started in Commodity Futures Trading*. The plan should consider the degree of risk to be undertaken, the tax objectives (a trader has to hold a profitable long position in futures only six months to achieve long-term gain; holdings in the actual physical commodity require a year), the entry and exit points, the

number of positions to be taken, when to add or eliminate some or all of the positions, etc. Paramount in this plan is deciding risk exposure by prefixing stop-loss areas for longs and stop-loss buy areas for any shorts. After formulating the plan, put it into action in a riskless fashion.

6. Accomplish this by paper-trading in silver futures according to the plan for at least three months. Enter purchases and sales according to market conditions as if the orders had actually been executed. Paper trading seasons the trader to become accustomed to daily changes in equity and enables the budding trader to make any needed alterations as a result of such activity.

7. Keep accurate daily records religiously of the trading plan and its paper profits and losses so that this habit can continue when trading for real.

8. At the end of three months analyze the results and decide if the effort is worthwhile or if it can be comfortably handled in the light of any other acitivites you are involved in.

9. If it is found that executing a properly constructed trading plan and keeping regular track of the results is too time-consuming or strenuous, seek out an experienced, well-trained account executive at a firm interested in accommodating speculators. Such firms are members of major exchanges and members of the Futures Industry Association. A letter to that association at 1919 Pennyslvania Avenue, N.W., Washington, D.C. 20006 will bring you a listing of member firms who participate in such activity.

5. SILVER OPTIONS

At the present writing the only sensible silver option is the one covering 1,000 ounces, issued and guaranteed by Mocatta Metals, and vended under stringent rules of the CFTC through authorized agents. Such agents include giant firms like Merrill, Lynch; Bache; Conti; Shearson, etc. These options, most popular in the form of calls, give the purchaser the right to call upon Mocatta during the last five days of the involved term of the option 1,000 ounces of triple nine silver at the contract price (strike price) agreed on the option. Thus, if September silver is trading at $16 an ounce and the risk-taker decides to buy an option at that strike price, a premium in money is paid for the right of the holder to acquire 1,000 ounces of silver at $16 an ounce during the last four trading days in August and the first trading day in September, when the option will die or be abandoned if it has not been exercised (the silver is demanded and paid for) or resold.

The saving feature of the Mocatta silver option is that the metals firm makes a two-way market normally in its offerings. If in the third week in July, September silver stood at $16 an ounce and a $16 strike September silver option (call) were offered by Mocatta, the premium would be about $1,903. And if, the same day—with the silver price unchanged—the buyer wanted to sell it back to Mocatta, he would receive $1,213. The difference between the bid and the asked on a Mocatta option is the "spread." For many years, when silver acted gently in the marketplace like an old gelding, the spread between the bids and the asked of Mocatta options was quite close and reasonable. After the silver market began to surge in 1979, the spread between what Mocatta wanted to charge for its options and what it would pay on resale began to widen like crazy. At one point in 1979 I prohibited purchase of new Mocatta options at Conti because of the widening spreads. But since the silver market has quilted in the wake of the Hunt fiasco, the silver option spreads have come down quite a bit, and there is no need for such a restriction. One thing is certain about purchase of a Mocatta silver call, and that is that the buyer cannot lose more than the cost of the involved option.

When the silver option used to cover 10,000 ounces, a trader could purchase such an option and go short two Comex or CBOT contracts, knowing that if he were wrong about the market—and it rose—the most he could lose was the cost of buying the options and the costs of the round-turn commissions at the clearing member for the futures.

But on September 12, 1979, Dr. Jarecki changed things a bit. The size of the silver option went to 5,000 ounces, and, subsequently, in 1980 was reduced to 1,000 ounces. Thus, for a trader to use Mocatta options to protect one Comex or CBOT short contract, he would have to purchase five silver calls and thereupon pay five commissions (we assume the premium for 5,000 ounces is precisely five times that of 1,000 ounces, but, of course, our presumptions might be wrong).

Understandably at this writing, therefore, the Comex and the CBOT have applied to reduce their contracts to 1,000 ounces so that a trader can protect himself completely during the life of an existing call if he buys only one Mocatta call in the case where the Comex contract will be only 1,000 ounces.

In addition to silver calls, a trader can also purchase Mocatta silver puts. In this case the puts can be used as speculative vehicles, hoping that silver will fall. If the speculator is wrong and the price of silver soars, the most the luckless speculator can lose is the cost of the silver puts. Or if the trader is indeed bullish on silver but fears the sudden arrival of renewed liquidation in the physicals market because of selling from either the Hunts or Saudi Arabia, the trader can protect acquired long positions in futures contracts by purchasing silver puts. If the market collapses, the trader in effect has presold his positions in futures at the strike price of the puts less the cost of the purchased puts. If the price of silver rises, the trader will lose all the money he invested in the puts but will profit further on the silver positions. In effect, the silver long is insured for the life of the puts.

Mocatta now must vend its options through selected dealers, including some high mark-up firms like International Precious Metals of Florida and International Trading Group of New York, to name two. This system will change when and if CFTC ever fulfills the mandate conferred on it by Congress to initiate exchange-traded options. If that happens, the market for options should be much more liquid, prices will be quoted in the daily newspapers, and chances are that the cost of trading options would decline.

In addition to the actual premium required for any Mocatta option, a purchaser now has to pay a brokerage fee to the authorized agent firm vending the options. Conti charges the lowest commission, because sales of such options are merely an accommodation for customers who request them. Conti makes no effort to market these options at all. Merrill Lynch, Shearson, and Bache charge 5 percent or more of the option premiums to the buyers and again may charge similar or reduced fees to the sellers.*

Therefore, before buying any Mocatta silver options it pays to shop around. It is sincerely hoped that the CFTC will some day soon inaugurate trading in metal options on the exchanges, but after all the trouble the agency has had with the silver situation earlier in 1980, chances are that if such options make their debut, they will cover only gold.

Another form of limited-risk trading in silver involves the so-called limited-risk-forward delivery silver contract or, put another way, simply silver leverage contract.

6. LEVERAGE CONTRACTS

For most of the first three years the employees of the CFTC were kept quite busy chasing what their late chairman claimed were "options crooks." Since the options ban on "foreign" LME and London Terminal Options went into effect in June 1978, the expanded staff of the CFTC has been busy chasing the "leverage crooks."

Some very innovative thinkers realized years ago that the Commodity Futures Trading Commission had no power over cash commodities, and they promptly devised a forward contract containing a limited-risk provision. In other words, the scam involves sending money for the forward purchase

---

* A copy of *A Short Course in Mocatta Options* is available by writing the author care of the publisher of this book.

in August 1979, of, say, silver at 10 percent in 1,000-ounce lots to be delivered to the customer in January 1980. The potential sucker is convinced over the phone by boiler room salesmen that for a mere $6,000 he will make millions when silver goes to 100. The sucker sends money and gets a confirmation showing he bought 1,000 ounces of silver in August deliverable in January, and at that time he has to pay $10,000 for the 1,000 ounces of 99.9 silver if he wants delivery. Of course, if the price has declined and the leverage contract holder does not desire to possess the silver, why that's perfectly fine with the seller of the contracts, and the buyer loses his up-front money. But hold. Such a contract entered into in August at $10 for $6,000 has become valuable in October when silver is $17. At that point the salesman calls and suggests the holder "roll over" the successful leverage contract into another one going out much further, till, say, July 1980, etc. Of course, for this service the sucker has only to send another $6,000.

When silver in January rises toward $50, the holder, who has already sunk $12,000 into an options substitute, calls up to sell back his leverage contract for at least $50,000. "Sorry," a recorded message tells him when he phones the leverage contracting firm, "we are closed. We have gone out of business. . . ."

From the growing list of indictments anent leverage contracts issued by marginal firms in anything from cash silver to sugar to heating oil to gold, we have come to a very arbitrary and biased conclusion by warning everyone to steer clear of such contracts—and rigidly avoid them. Remember: *Caveat emptor* wasn't only for the Romans.

7. SILVER SHARES

While fortunes have been made and lost in trading silver physicals and futures, let alone options, few securities on the New York Stock Exchange have ever performed like those of companies in 1979 and 1980 owning interests in silver mining or processing. The most outstanding silver issue of all turned out to be Hecla Mining, the stock on the big board that had the largest percentage upward move during 1979.

In December 1978 I gave a talk at the Northwest Mining Association annual convention in Spokane, Washington, where men who are men and women who are perhaps often better than men meet and drink moose milk for breakfast (half milk, half scotch). At dinner on the night of my arrival Phil Lindstrom confided that I ought to buy some shares in Hecla, then trading at 4⅝. I agreed, but first asked him to tell me how much I would earn for 1978?

"Earn?" he chuckled in his disarming manner. "We're going to have a write-off this year of an aborted copper venture in Arizona, and we're going to lose about $96 million, or a loss of about $13 a share."

Now how could I possibly, as a supposedly smart investor, risk my after-tax money in a company that intended to have a $96 million loss? I didn't buy any stock in Hecla and watched it subsequently soar into the twenties during 1979. Sure enough, in December 1979, when silver traded at about the $20 level, I again went to Spokane to give a talk to the same hardy, honest mining people, whose motto is simply "Keep on Mucking."

This time I blithely confessed what a silver dummy I was about not buying any Hecla at 4⅝ and pointed out that Hecla had done even better than the silver it mines by trading at $24 a share when silver wavered at about the $20 level. In answer to a question about where silver and Hecla are going in the eighties, I conjured up Bunker Hunt's prediction that the gold/silver ratio, then about 20 to 1, would drop to 5 to 1. With gold at about $400, that put silver at about $80 an ounce, and my answer was: "Silver is going to 80 in the eighties, and Hecla, which has led the silver price, could go to to 88 in the eighties."

Again I did not buy any Hecla stock, since the mining company still had not earned any money because of the severe write-off of the Arizona copper thing. About a month after I got back to New York, where was Hecla stock? At 53!

What I have tried to point out is that there are stocks, such as Hecla Mining, that go along with the silver price and can be fine investments for growth-minded young people.

Another issue I favor on the big board is Asarco, actually the largest silver producer in the United States. Engelhard Minerals, also on the NYSE, is another growth company, especially as long as it harbors shrewd traders like Ray Nessim of Philipp Brothers, who serves as first vice-chairman of Comex.

The tripling of the silver price during the past year has caused a stirring of interest in abandoned silver mines, in properties that could hardly be profitably developed when silver stood at $1 an ounce, but might be money-makers at $20 an ounce. Nowhere on earth has this speculative fever developed as it has in the Pacific Northwest. Stocks with fancy-sounding names like Silver Dollar and Silver Syndicate rose in price as speculators leaped into the silver shares fray. A listing from the Spokane newspaper of what these mining companies were in 1979 and what they went for in July 1980 appears on page 158.

Whether or not many of these so-called mining shares will ever become sources of silver, even if silver rises to $100 an ounce, is highly debatable. But 1,000 shares of a dollar stock costs only $1,000, and that's the most the risk-taker can lose. A thousand shares of a 20-cent stock costs only $200.

I confess readily that though I did not plunge into Hecla because of being strapped every year for tax money, I managed to take a flyer in some low-priced, "penny" Spokane silver stocks. There are also some stocks covering silver mining interests that are not listed on exchanges, but are, instead, traded over-the-counter.

Shannon Pratt is a well-known expert in this area, and an up-to-date listing of silver OTC stocks can be obtained by writing to him at 534 S.W. 3rd Avenue, Portland, Oregon 97204.

The big difference, of course, between speculating in over-the-counter silver shares and in trading in silver futures is

SPOKANE STOCK EXCHANGE

Stock	Price July 25, 1979	Price July 25, 1980
Allied	18–23c	85–95c
Calahn	$19.25–20	$26–27
Clayton	68–78c	$2.30–2.50
Day Mn	$12.50–13.25	$30–31
4th of July	6–9c	11–15
Gladstn	$1.50–1.75	$1–1.25
Grandvw	6–9c	7–10c
Gulf R	$14.25–15	$25–26
Hecla	$13.25–14	$36.50–37.50
Helena Sil	6–10c	18–25c
Hmstk	$32.50–33.50	$67–68
Indpnd	43–50c	58–65c
Li'l Squaw	62–70c	$1.55–1.75
Met M & L	7–10c	14–16c
Metropltn	$1.55–1.75	$3.25–3.50
Mineral Mt	12–15c	41–50c
New Hilr	2–3c	5–10c
ONB	$19–20	$22–23
Princetn	9–12c	24–30c
Quad Mtls	18–25c	13–18
Rego	$6.25–7	$6–6.50
Sidney	10–13c	30–35c
Silv Butte	14–18	24–64c
Sil Dir	$5.75–6.25	$13.25–14
Sil Ledge	6–9c	20–25c
Silvr Mt	19–25c	61–65c
Sunsh	$14–14.50	$14–15
Sun Con	$1.50–1.80	$3.90–4.20
WWP	$22.75–23.50	$19.50–20.50
West Gld	12–15c	30–35c
Western Sil	10–15c	21–25c
Western A	20–30c	28–33c

that there can never be a margin call, and the risk-taker knows in advance how much can be lost by sensibly limiting the amount of money risked in speculative shares.

8. SILVER SPREADS

One of the many different definitions of the word "spread" involves the word "feast," such as a spread set for a sumptuous meal. The dictionary does not define spread in the sense that the word is used in futures markets, but it does define straddle in one sense as "to buy in one market and sell short in another," and a straddle as "the state of being long in one market and short in another."

But what the dictionary omits is that in the futures markets the word spread is the *synonym* of straddle—only it isn't as simple as it sounds. For example, there are four major types of spreads:

1. Intramarket spreads.
2. Intermarket spreads.
3. Interproduct spreads.
4. Interrelated spreads.

Naturally, innovative traders can categorize other types of spreads until the possibilities boggle the mind. But before entering into a description of the major kinds of spreads, it is fitting first to define them.

An intramarket spread in silver involves buying one contract month and simultaneously selling another delivery month on the same exchange and in the same commodity, in this case, of course, silver. Thus, if a trader decided to put on a Comex silver spread, the order might read, "buy one September silver and sell one December silver" (either at market or at a fixed preset differential). Since the order involves the purchase of a silver futures contract on Comex and simultaneous sale of a Comex silver contract for a differing month, it is an *intramarket spread.*

An intermarket spread may involve the purchase of a December Comex silver contract and the simultaneous sale of a December CBOT contract. Since the commodity involved is silver on both futures contracts, but the order is executed on two different exchanges, the product is called an *inter-market spread*.

An interproduct spread would be the purchase of silver for September delivery on Comex and the simultaneous sale of January silver coin bags on the New York Mercantile Exchange. In this case, the coins contain 90 percent silver, and it is valid to say that the coins are primarily made from silver, plus minor amounts of other metals. Since the spread involves the primary substance, and the product of that substance, it is called an *interproduct spread*.

The final major category of silver spreads involves relationships between silver and other commodities. It is well known that there is a correlationship of quite a close nature between the movements of silver and gold. If gold rises, silver should also rise, although perhaps to varying degrees. If gold declines, silver likewise should normally decline, although again perhaps not to the same degree. In recent years technicians and various other systems-makers have related the movement of silver to platinum, to copper, and even to soybeans.

Some years ago Bunker Hunt, who since 1973 has been bending under the burden of carrying huge stocks of silver physicals, became interested in accumulating soybeans. Although there may have been times when the Hunts have been temporarily strapped for cash, there can be little dispute that the family possesses a private stockpile of silver. So it seemed perfectly natural for Bunker to offer to pay for the soybeans slated to be delivered to him some years ago with silver rather than cash. As a result, traders began to notice a correlation between the movements of silver and the movements of the soybean futures prices. Thus, if a trader purchased November beans and simultaneously sold December Comex silver (or vice versa), such a spread would be termed an *interrelated spread*.

With this bit of background in what silver spreads of various nature might be, it would be fitting to go on and discuss how they are used. But before doing this it is proper to define the word *butterfly*.

Many years ago Charley Mattey of Bache happened to be in deep discussion with some of his staff about a method of smoothing out the obvious price risks involved in simple spreads, and an innovation termed a "butterfly" was born. In this ploy the spreader buys a near month in silver and one contract of a far month, and simultaneously sells two silver contracts in a middle-term month. By so doing, the chances of the spreader losing a lot of money—if conditions affecting the delivery months change radically—are minimized. At the same time, the chances for profit using butterflies are radically reduced. But in all cases the spreader who puts on butterflies or spreads in silver assumes plenty of risk, and plenty of chance for loss.

And now for a brief explanation of spreading with silver futures contracts:

A. Intramarket Spreads

Under normal market conditions the silver futures contracts in both Chicago and New York trade in a contango pattern. That is, the near months trade at lower prices than the farther-out months because, theoretically, someone is "carrying" (owns, finances, and stores) the silver that eventually has to be delivered if the silver long remains in the contract through the delivery month. The differences, therefore, between what the September, December, and March Comex silver contracts trade at, for example, are more or less mathematically determined by the cost of money (going interest rates, usually the T-Bill rate). On page 162 you will find a table of closing silver futures prices on the New York Comex as of July 25, 1980

In July 1980 a spreader might be interested in using the most popularly traded months for such a purpose: September and December 1980. Notice that the difference between

SILVER (NYCX)

5,000 troy oz.; ¢ per troy oz.

Hi	Lo	Mo.	Hi	Lo	Close	Net Chge.	Open Int.
4240.00	642.40	Jul.	1668.0	1645.0	1668.0	+ 31.0	103
1755.00	1330.00	Aug.	1669.0	1650.0	1669.0	+ 27.0	51
4280.00	666.00	Sep.	1685.0	1648.0	1684.0	+ 31.0	6632
4437.00	796.00	Dec.	1735.0	1700.0	1731.0	+ 32.0	5095
4183.00	843.50	Jan.	1755.0	1740.0	1747.5	+ 33.5	1792
4493.50	924.00	Mar.	1790.0	1750.0	1779.0	+ 35.0	4266
4530.50	1006.00	May	1815.0	1790.0	1811.5	+ 37.5	2390
4357.00	1229.00	Jul.	1854.0	1843.5	1843.5	+ 39.5	1569
4200.00	1254.00	Sep.	......	......	1875.5	+ 41.5	642
4140.00	1340.00	Dec.	......	......	1923.5	+ 44.4	101
4164.00	4164.00	Jan.	......	......	1939.5	+ 45.5	327
2092.00	885.00	Mar.	1971.5	1948.0	1971.5	+ 47.5	755
2092.00	1943.00	May	......	......	2003.5	+ 49.5	325

Est. sales 1,200; sales Thur. 2,518.
Total open interest Thur. 24,097 up 49 from Wed.

the two deliveries amounted at that time to 47 cents, so the December contract was at a premium to the September contract of 47 cents an ounce. Will this premium widen to, say, 60 cents or narrow to 30 cents? That is the question the spreader must answer in the attempt to seek profits with such a spread.

Why should the relationship between the September delivery and the December delivery month prices change?

The answer lies in several directions, chiefly: (1) interest rates; and (2) trading interest.

In the first instance, if interest rates rise, then the premium of December over September should logically widen (go out), since it costs more to carry the physical silver. If interest rates keep declining, then the spreads will narrow (come in). If the spreader has been properly positioned (has bought the right month and sold the right month), a profit will ensue. If the spreader has done a Corrigan (gone the wrong way), a loss, of course, results.

The second important aspect of spreading involves trading interest. This may be defined as the "action" in any specific silver future. Obviously, the action in the far-out months is not nearly as pronounced as the volume of buying and selling of nearby contracts. So that on any specific trading day the spreader might encounter keen interest in one of the months, but almost a total lack of trading interest in the other. As a result, the person or firm who accepts the market position opposing the spreader may take the business on distorted terms. Such terms may make it difficult for the spreader to effect a future profit.

There are several reasons why spreading in silver has become quite popular over the years. The reasons involve: (1) commissions for the service people handling the account (once a spread is put on, it has to be rolled over and/or unwound; and (2) tax implications.

In the first instance a spread, while reducing the obvious risk to the speculator of simply being long or short an outright silver contract, utilizes much less margin and generates much more commissions on the money required to launch the spread than the margins required or the commissions generated in an outright long or short.

In the second case the intelligent use of silver spreading permitted tax management to the degree that an investor who had established (or intended to establish) massive capital gains in a tax year could defer those gains to a future year— he had simply to wipe off most or all of the gains by establishing a loss in silver for one year and simultaneously locking up a profit for the following year, etc. Of course, such "tax straddlers" then became hooked into the situation and obviously had to expand their efforts in silver spreads with each passing year. For example, if an investor gained $50,000 in short-term trading in a calendar year and had no other offsetting capital losses of a short-term nature, the risk-taker could buy a September and sell a December silver for the following year, and just before the current year ended close out whichever leg of the September/December silver spread represented loss. By estimating how volatile silver might be between the time the tax spreads were contemplated and the time something might have to be done, the spreader could calculate roughly how many spreads would have to be put on to effect wiping off all or most of the $50,000 short-term gain for the current calendar year. Assuming that the short side of the spread contract reflected loss, on the last possible day of the year the spreader would buy-in the December contract at a loss and roll it over by going short the January or March of the succeeding year, etc.

But there never exists any assurance to the spreader that a massive monetary loss might not ensue when all the spreads eventually are unwound. Again this loss could occur because of changed interest rates, or because the difference in prices between the months made no economic sense.

Spreading is also used by some traders to lock in a position. For example, a trader decided silver earlier in 1980 would rise, and just after January 1 put on some longs. As the price rose toward the $50 pinnacle, the trader may have become a bit nervous and gone short any of the back months. By doing this, he "locked-in" profits on the longs and insured against the collapse that eventually arrived.

When making an attempt to profit by spreading silver, it should be recognized that there are two distinct kinds of silver spreads: (1) bull spreads; and (2) bear spreads. In a bull spread the back month is sold and a front month (nearby month) is purchased. In a bear spread the trader sells the front month and buys the back month. The rationale behind this is simply that the spreader expects both interest rates and market conditions to change. If there is an exceedingly tight nearby supply of silver, then the near months should advance faster than the back months and decline slower than the back months. If there is a plentiful supply of silver in the warehouses and bullion dealer inventories, but chances for the future supply may be dimmed because of possible strikes or transport problems, then the nearby months will rise slower than the back months in a rising silver market and fall faster than the back months in a declining silver market.

Thus, depending on how the spreader sees both interest rates and silver inventories going, silver spreads would be bought (bull spreads) or sold (bear spreads).

Like many aspects of accountancy, silver spreading, though based on numbers, also requires correct judgment and the ability to execute the spreads sensibly and in the right direction. Spreading opportunities arise every now and then because of stress conditions on the silver exchanges—shorts are forced to cover because of inability to produce variation margins in a rising silver market, or longs are compelled to liquidate because of their inability to add equity margins in a falling silver market. In the event of such happenings, the chances are that spreaders may be able to enter the market in an unusually favorable manner, providing they can gauge what will happen to the following: (1) the price of silver for the next year or so; (2) the course of the prime rate during the next year or so; and (3) the amount of speculative interest that will accrue to the silver markets in the next year or so. Aside from these factors, the chances of making money with spreads depends strictly on the management of the spreads after they have been instituted.

B. Intermarket Spreads

Although the risks of spreading in an intramarket fashion are obvious to both neophyte and the experienced trader, the risks of an intermarket spread may be greatly lessened because of the arbitrage involved. Naturally, not every trader has the ability or the facilities to execute orders in the pits of Chicago and New York simultaneously, or perhaps execute orders in New York, Chicago, and on the LME in London all at the same time. But some traders do have such facilities—and the ability—to monitor and execute orders to buy and sell the same thing for the same or differing delivery times—with a built-in, and guaranteed, profit, because the intermarket spread has been put on in such a manner that receipt and delivery are contemplated or the conditions of settlement are already built in in favor of the spreader.

For example, purchase of spot silver in London and simultaneous sale for nearby or future month delivery in Chicago or New York are the most common forms of such arbitrage—and are accomplished mostly by bullion dealers and their traders. Another form of intermarket spread involves buying in New York or Comex and simultaneously selling in Chicago, and vice versa. In any event, the spreader who uses such arbitrage may tie up a lot of capital to make very little money, but arbitrage is never a losing game like bull or bear spreading.

C. Interproduct Spreads

The most prevalent interproduct spread in silver involves the purchase of silver futures on Comex or CBOT and the simultaneous sale of silver coin bag futures on the New York Mercantile Exchange, or vice versa.

The drawbacks of such spreading involves: (1) the lack of trading interest in the silver coin bag contracts; and (2) the obvious difficulty—even if there were sufficient trading interest in bag contracts—of converting the coin bags into triple nine Comex-grade silver delivery bars. Moreover, since the silver coins packed into the bags are in circulated condition, the chances of having a perfect arbitrage by envisioning the meltdown of the coins into bars at an optimum is doubtful indeed.

Another drawback of such spreading involves margins. Since two clearinghouses are involved (the New York Merc and Comex or CBOT), separate margins must be deposited in such spreads as if they were unrelated and outright longs and shorts on differing commodities, instead of a long and short in silver and a product made mainly from silver.

So before effecting any spreads of this nature, it pays to determine in advance what the margins will be at the clearing member handling the account.

Other interproduct spreads involve the sale of Comex futures by bullion dealers against attic silver (mostly sterling of 92.5 percent or better purity) or silver coins the bullion dealer may be repurchasing from holders of physical bags who decide to sell them back into the market place.

D. Interrelated Market Spreads

The most popular interrelated spread involves gold and silver. As previously noted, the free world ratio between one ounce of gold and the number of ounces of silver required to purchase that one ounce of gold averaged for almost a hundred years 32/1. In 1979 and early 1980 the price of silver moved much faster than gold, and the ratio dropped toward 15/1. After Silver Thursday the ratio rose toward 40/1, and many experts believe it will remain in that area for years to come.

But not Bunker Hunt. He and his brother Herbert believe silver is way too low in relationship to the current gold price.

Bunker still insists the gold/silver ratio will someday be 5/1. If this turns out to be true, spreaders can make a fortune by shorting gold and buying silver.

It then does not matter whether gold goes to $1,000 an ounce or drops to $300 an ounce. If the ratio narrows toward the 5/1 area, the spreader who has gone short gold and gone long silver will be able to buy a few oil properties on his own. If, on the other hand, the ratio does not narrow, but continues instead to widen and increase toward 50/1, then the spreader, who has envisioned a shrinkage of the gold/silver ratio, will lose a lot of money.

No matter what happens, the spreader can at any time close out that part of the ratio that is worsening and go with the trend. The same, of course, can be done with any of the other spreads. The spreader can "leg it" or "lift one of the legs." The long side and the short side of any simple spread are in the parlance of futures trading called "legs." So, for example, if a spreader went long one September Comex silver at $16.84 and simultaneously went short one September Comex gold at $658.50, he could close out whichever side of this spread happened to go the wrong way in the weeks to come and remain with the side that seemed to be heading in a profitable direction.

Of course, after the spreader lifts one leg of a spread, the remaining leg is exposed to the risks and the margins of an outright position.

Spreading then may be summed up as an approach to commodity futures speculation with a lessened degree of risk than outright futures trading. But in sacrificing risk the spreader also sacrifices much of the chance for leveraged profits involved in assuming those risks in the first place.

Here are some do's and dont's for potential silver spreaders:

SILVER SPREADING DO'S

1. Study intensely the mathematical relationships between the delivery months on Comex and CBOT day-by-day for the past three years.

2. Study interest rates and their changes for the past three years (use T-Bill interest rates).

3. Relate the changes in interest rates to the changes between the delivery months in order to become familiar with what happens to the silver prices in differing months when such changes occur.

4. After sufficient study, paper trade for the next three months with silver spreads devised by yourself in the light of what you think may happen to both the silver price and T-Bill rates.

SILVER SPREADING DONT'S

1. Do not put on any kind of silver spreads if you don't understand the risks and rewards involved.

2. Do not spread silver for profits using anything except simple intramarket approaches.

3. Do not effect silver spreads unless either you know what you are doing or have been properly advised and understand completely what steps you are taking, and why.

4. Do not open or maintain a silver spreading account at any firm not a member of both Comex and CBOT.

5. Do not overspread. If you begin to make money with silver spreads, don't go whole hog. If you lose at the beginning, don't throw good money after bad.

Among the beneficiaries of the rapid silver decline during March were members of the Comex board, such as M. Marx and Irving Redel, who had massive spread positions and who were able to profit subsequently from those positions because the silver longs were compelled to liquidate or roll over their own positions.

*

TEN

*

THE SILVER FUTURE

While the wars waged loudly in the silver pits between the silver longs and the shorts in 1979 and the first quarter of 1980, the rising price of silver raised havoc in many industrial areas.

The greatest use of silver, of course, is in photography, and Eastman Kodak is the world's largest user. Normally the giant camera company resorts to buying hedges in silver futures covering silver it intends to purchase. But with the inexorable rise in price during 1979 Kodak did not enter the futures markets for hedging purposes in the usual manner. And the company did not raise the price of its products until late in 1979 when it became compelled to plan for its silver stockpile for 1980.

Du Pont, a giant chemical company, which has made significant inroads into X-ray photography, managed to use innovation and reduce the amount of silver needed for such applications.

Manufacturers of sterling silverware were damaged the most, in retrospect, because their products normally contain 92.5 percent or more silver, and to pay prices of $20 an ounce or more would make the place settings of sterling rather prohibitive for newlyweds and young marrieds.

But the rising price of silver created a tremendously effective cash-flow for the old marrieds, widows and widowers, and heirs.

Silverware, flatware, loving cups, track medals, even teeth that contained fillings—some with blood still on the roots—were taken out of the attic, the cellar, and even the mouth, and transported to the nearest silver-scrap collection depot.

The stream of so-called "attic silver" created a silver pipeline that grew daily as the price rose.

Innovative shoppers quickly found that the department stores in many cities and smaller jewelry and gift stores in suburban areas paid scant attention to the silver price in London or on Comex and were retailing merchandise made of silver at prices hardly reflecting the rise. One college student purchased all the sterling place settings in a Pennsylvania store at bargain prices, and later, when silver soared, sold them back to the store at much higher prices.

In December 1979, an innovative Canadian discovered that Holt Renfrew, a Montreal-based department store, was advertising gift certificates in the form of one-ounce silver medallions at $25 each, in Canadian currency, of course, which was then at a discount of about 15 percent from the U.S. dollar. The market price of silver was then about $24 an ounce, U.S., or the equivalent of about $28 Canadian, so the medallions were priced about $3 below their value as silver. "As calmly as I could," said this Canadian, "I bought twenty, and then told the clerk I could use some more. There were 167, and I bought them all."

During the next double handful of days he surreptitiously picked up 1,273 from the Montreal and Toronto stores. Because he didn't want to arouse suspicion, he managed to enlist friends and relatives to make the purchases, paying them a "commission."

Later he sold off 1,085 of the medallions for prices ranging from $40 to $52, and garnered a profit of $10,552, in Canadian money. The other 355 pieces he decided to keep as a hedge against future inflation.

Traditionally, gold has been considered over the past five thousand years as one of the best hedges against inflation. Silver has been hoarded in India for hundreds of years as a "money of last resort." But since the Hunts entered the picture back in 1973 and since the Saudis have been accumulating it during 1979 and 1980, there can be little question that silver will be increasingly purchased in its various forms as inflation hedges all over the world.

Last year Franz Pick, who has been crying gloom and doom for paper money almost as long as this writer has been in the markets, suddenly decided to pick silver as the best inflation hedge for the 1980s. While his debatable and repetitious prediction that the U.S. will have to reverse split its paper currency and some day back it with gold is quite well known in writings and Pick speeches, I cannot help agreeing with him when it comes to silver.

Why will silver's price inexorably rise and gradually overtake the gold price?

To answer this it is fitting to dwell on the current conditions of supply and demand of silver around the world. Ever since 1946 there has been an annual deficit between the number of ounces of new silver that comes from mineral ores and the number of ounces used in the free world.

In the United States, the most silver-hungry nation in the world, we use approximately 160 million ounces of silver a year and mine about 40 million. So there is a deficit between supply and demand of about 120 million ounces.

How is this deficit filled?

The answer is from scrap, from coin melt, from silver recovery in photography, and other forms of recycling. It is also filled handily by purchase from our neighbors, Canada, Mexico, and Peru.

Since Canada produces just about what we do in silver each year—if there are no strikes—and since its smaller population consumes far less, Canada has an annual surplus of silver to sell. The same is true of Peru. That sparsely populated nation, rich in minerals, produces about 40 million silver ounces a year—again when there are no strikes—and uses a sliver of this supply, selling the rest.

Mexico occasionally mints silver coins, and in 1979 boasted it would produce 60 million ounces of newly mined silver. But setting a production target is one thing and keeping it is something else. Mexico came in with about 47 million ounces in 1979.

What country, then, is the world's largest silver produces? The answer is the USSR.

Last year the Soviet Union mined more than 49 million ounces of silver from secondary ores. The USSR is not blessed with the kind of primary silver ores that lie deep beneath the earth in the Cœur d'Alene region of Idaho. Instead, silver is found as a secondary product in lead, zinc, and copper ores.

While many government agencies in the United States are well aware of how much silver the Soviets produce annually, no agency, including the CIA, seems to have thought it important to determine the extent of annual Soviet silver demand.

I estimated how much silver the Soviets use by doing a demographic approach to the problem.

I determined that Soviet citizens have become more and more westernized since Khrushchev banged his shoes on the U.N. table and later "retired." This westernization includes extensive use of X-rays, even for minor injuries, a growing interest by Soviet citizens in taking pictures of children, grandchildren, sweethearts, wives, even pets and flowers.

Consequently, there is a growing demand for silver in the Soviet Union as the country gears up for "defense" by using silver batteries instead of lithium chloride substitutes, as we do in our missiles. Silver in the Soviet Union is also increasingly needed for computer and other electronic applications. Briefly, then, since the Soviet population exceeds 300 million people, I calculated that they did not use as much as the ¾ ounce of silver per year that Americans seem to use. Instead, my estimate involves about ½ ounce of silver per Soviet person per year, or a demand of about 150 million ounces.

Since the Soviets have long since recycled whatever czarist silver and samovars are not in museums, their silver scrap supply has just about disappeared. Granted that a modicum of silver is recovered from recycling of photographic supplies and used batteries, there still exists a significant annual Soviet silver shortfall—and the shortfall keeps increasing. To meet their annual silver demand, therefore, the Soviets will eventually have to resort to free world commodity markets, including the LME, Comex, and CBOT to hedge against their burgeoning silver needs. Unhampered by the red tape required in the United States for our government to purchase or sell silver intelligently by managing our national strategic stockpile, the USSR can execute any plan devised to stockpile silver quietly and efficiently through the Swiss banks and other agents.

It naturally follows that as the Soviet Union becomes more and more westernized, and as it beefs up its defenses from missiles to computers, its need for more and more silver will cause upward pressure on world markets.

In the meantime, despite American ingenuity at finding substitutes when the price of a commodity rises above reason, it will be exceedingly difficult to substitute for silver in many critical applications.

Therefore, the 1980s will see an invisible—and perhaps someday visible—silver war between the forces of capitalism, led by the United States and the forces of communism, led by the Soviet Union. This trade war will basically involve silver; and the countries that hold the trump cards are Canada, Mexico, and Peru.

While it is likely that Canada will continue to supply silver to the United States in such a situation, the same cannot be said with assurance for Mexico and Peru.

Both these nations have exhibited occasional political instability and are subject to revolutions sponsored by communism or its agents. Both of these countries normally do business with the highest bidder— and as the Soviets get . strapped for silver during the coming decade, they can resort to the same tactics with Mexico and Peru that worked in Cuba.

For example, when sugar traded at about 6 cents a pound on the world market, the USSR paid Cuba about 40 cents a pound. No one, of course, knows what the Soviet Union charged the Cubans when they needed goods formerly bought from Americans.

South American countries have little regard for such contrivances as the grain embargo ordered by President Carter to attempt to punish the Soviets for setting foot in Afghanistan, a country that had surrendered to them two years before. The Soviets were undeterred. They filled most of their grain needs in Argentina. What the President accomplished was simply to shift the business out of the United States to other countries.

Will the Soviets need silver during the next decade as badly as they will grain?

I think their needs in this direction are already critical, since they were buying silver during the summer and fall of 1979 in the world market places and could very well return as buyers before the end of 1980.

History often repeats itself, and perhaps that is what's wrong with history. Some years ago (1973 and 1974) the Japanese needed copper, and their purchases in the markets of London and New York caused copper to climb to heights rarely seen in history. When the Japanese stopped buying, the price of copper went into the tank. In 1978 the Soviets entered the lead markets through the LME, and the price of lead, long linked to the price of zinc and trading at about the same level as zinc, went bananas. When the Soviets exited from the LME lead market, the price of the metal dropped like a stone.

Could history repeat itself in the silver market?

If gold rose to $1,000 and silver rose concomitantly to trade at the normal 32 to 1 gold/silver ratio that existed for almost a hundred years before the silver war of 1979–80 in the silver pits, then silver should trade close to the $32 level.

Forecasting in many instances is like spitting in the wind. But I sincerely believe, in the light of the fundamentals, that if gold gets to $1,000 an ounce, the gold/silver ratio will be closer to 20 to 1 than 32 to 1. This will make a silver price of at least $50 a ounce.

Where would silver be if we give credence to Bunker Hunt's repeated prediction that the ratio will sink some day to 5 to 1? At $1,000 an ounce for gold, that's $200 an ounce for silver.

Can silver and gold both go into a decline that will bring them back to prices that existed before Jimmy Carter decided to cater to OPEC?

There could possibly be a decline in the prices of precious metals if an American Administration would do something constructive about stopping inflation. All of us have been unwitting victims of the ludicrous cosmetics of the Administration. We have seen it try to stop a worsening cost-push inflation with occasional doses of monetary medicine, by twisting up interest rates to destroy the longs in March, then unleashing the money supply when the prime rate collapsed in May after the longs were sold out—only partly, I should say.

In the meantime, the price of silver, like that of gold, will continue to fluctuate, and there will again be opportunity to seek profits in silver from a bullish posture. In the light of the increasing westernization of third world countries and China, I certainly would not ever be short of silver either in futures or physicals.

Imagine what would happen if cameras and film were purchased and used extensively throughout Africa and Asia? That time may not be too far distant, according to some sources. And if this happens, silver demand will again explode.

Finally, permit me to divulge something about do-it-yourself silver research. Many factors affect the silver price, and some firms spend millions digging for facts and figures upon which to make trading or hedging decisions. The small speculator does not have the sources to monitor the silver statistics, but free information is available at almost any large brokerage house that is a member of Comex or CBOT. Some of the larger firms maintain commodity research departments, such as the one I direct.

In this regard we approach the problem of profitable trading from the fundamental standpoint by examining production and consumption on a country-by-country and worldwide basis—and we also seek to find other fundamentals that may affect the prices of all precious metals, including silver. These may include interest rates, foreign exchange relationships, inflation levels, and the price of petroleum and its products. In seeking such information we examine many exhibits from many industry and trade sources, as well as making our own field trips and assessments.

Here is a detailed study of mine production of silver in 1979—with projections for 1980 through 1983:

MINE PRODUCTION OF SILVER

ON ACCOUNTABLE BASIS
IN MILLIONS OF TROY OUNCES

International Trade Countries	Actual		Projections		
	1978	1979	1980	1981	1982	1983

International Trade Countries	1978	1979	1980	1981	1982	1983
Countries producing more than 20 million troy ounces per year:						
Mexico	50.8	49.4	52.1	59.3	74.7	79.2
Peru	38.6	40.2	40.3	40.7	42.8	43.0
Canada	40.9	38.1	42.5	45.7	46.9	47.1
United States	38.9	37.1	39.8	42.8	49.2	49.3
Australia	23.1	24.8	26.5	26.0	28.1	29.8
Subtotal	192.3	189.6	201.2	214.5	241.7	248.4
Equivalent in metric tons	5,981	5,897	6,258	6,672	7,518	7,726
Change from previous year		−1%	+6%	+7%	+13%	+3%
Countries producing 1 million to 20 million troy ounces in 1979						
Japan	10.7	8.9	8.9	8.9	8.9	8.9
Chile	*8.2	8.3	8.3	9.3	10.5	10.5
Bolivia	6.0	5.7	5.8	5.9	5.9	5.9
Sweden	5.7	5.7	5.5	6.3	6.5	6.4
Yugoslavia	4.7	5.2	5.2	5.2	5.2	5.2
Spain	1.7	3.4	3.5	3.5	3.4	3.4
South Africa	3.1	3.2	6.4	6.4	6.4	6.5

MINE PRODUCTION OF SILVER (*continued*)
ON ACCOUNTABLE BASIS
IN MILLIONS OF TROY OUNCES

International Trade Countries	Actual			Projections		
	1978	1979	1980	1981	1982	1983
Zaire	2.9	2.9	3.2	3.1	2.2	2.4
South Korea	2.1	2.8	2.8	2.8	2.8	2.8
France	2.5	2.4	2.4	2.2	2.2	2.2
Morocco	2.2	2.4	2.4	2.4	2.4	2.4
Dominican Republic	1.8	2.3	1.7	1.7	1.7	1.7
Honduras	2.5	1.9	2.2	2.4	2.6	2.6
Philippines	2.0	1.8	2.2	2.2	2.2	2.2
Argentina	1.6	1.8	2.2	2.2	2.2	2.2
Greece	1.6	1.7	1.7	1.8	1.8	1.8
South West Africa	1.4	1.6	1.6	1.7	1.7	1.7
Papua New Guinea	1.7	1.4	1.4	1.3	1.4	1.4
Italy	1.2	1.1	1.1	1.1	1.1	1.1
Subtotal	*63.6	64.5	68.5	70.4	71.1	71.3
Equivalent in metric tons	*1,978	2,006	2,131	2,190	2,212	2,218
Change from previous year		+1%	+6%	+3%	+1%	0%

International Trade Countries	Actual		Projections			
	1978	1979	1980	1981	1982	1983
Countries producing less than 1 million troy ounces in 1979						
German Federal Republic	.85	1.04	.95	.95	.94	.94
Finland	.86	.80	.81	.77	.74	.75
Indonesia	.65	.79	.87	1.00	1.00	1.00
Ireland	.90	.74	.53	.77	.15	.15
Denmark (Greenland)	.56	.62	.58	.59	.58	.59
India	.43	.45	.45	.45	.45	.45
Nicaragua	.58	.32	.12	.12	.12	.12
Brazil	.30	.32	.28	.28	.28	.28
Burma	.37	.27	.41	.50	.58	.58
Tunisia	.23	.23	.23	.23	.23	.23
Turkey	.22	.22	.22	.22	.22	.22
El Salvador	.11	.20	.20	.20	.20	.20
Algeria	.10	.10	.10	.10	.10	.10
Rhodesia	.10	.10	.10	.10	.10	.10
Colombia	.05	.10	.10	.10	.10	.10
Taiwan	.09	.09	.08	.16	.19	.23
Zambia	.10	.08	.10	.10	.10	.10
Ecuador	.07	.07	.07	.07	.07	.07
Mauritania	.03	.03	.03	.03	.03	.03

MINE PRODUCTION OF SILVER (*continued*)
ON ACCOUNTABLE BASIS
IN MILLIONS OF TROY OUNCES

International Trade Countries	Actual		Projections			
	1978	1979	1980	1981	1982	1983
Portugal	.02	.03	.03	.03	.03	.03
Ghana	.02	.02	.02	.02	.02	.02
Kenya	.02	.02	.02	.02	.02	.02
Fiji	.02	.01	.01	.01	.01	.01
Guatemala	.01	.01	.01	.01	.01	.01
New Zealand	.01	.01	.01	.01	.01	.01
Tanzania	.01	.01	.01	.01	.01	.01
Great Britain	.01	.01	.01	.01	.01	.01
Subtotal	6.72	6.69	6.35	6.86	6.30	6.36
Equivalent in metric tons	209	208	198	213	196	198
Total International Trade Countries	*262.62	260.79	276.05	291.76	319.10	326.06
Equivalent in metric tons	*8,169	8,112	8,586	9,075	9,925	10,142
Change from previous year		−0.7%	+6%	+6%	+9%	+2%
Eastern Bloc Countries						
Soviet Union	*50.5	49.8	50.0	51.0	52.0	53.0
Poland	*21.9	23.0	24.5	24.5	24.5	24.5

International Trade Countries	Actual		Projections			
	1978	1979	1980	1981	1982	1983
China, People's Republic of	*1.5	2.0	2.0	2.0	2.0	2.0
North Korea	1.6	1.5	1.5	1.5	1.5	1.5
German Democratic Republic	1.5	1.5	1.5	1.5	1.5	1.5
Czechoslovakia	1.3	1.1	1.1	1.1	1.1	1.1
Romania	1.3	1.0	1.0	1.0	1.0	1.0
Bulgaria	1.0	0.8	0.8	0.8	0.8	0.8
Hungary	0.1	0.1	0.1	0.1	0.1	0.1
Total Eastern Bloc Countries	*80.7	80.8	82.5	83.5	84.5	85.5
Equivalent in metric tons	*2,510	2,513	2,566	2,597	2,628	2,659
Change from previous year		+0.1%	+2%	+1%	+1%	+1%
World Total	*343.32	341.59	358.55	375.26	403.60	411.56
Equivalent in metric tons	*10,679	10,625	11,152	11,672	12,554	12,801
Change from previous year		−0.5%	+5%	+5%	+8%	+2%

*Revised

These figures were supplied through the courtesy of the Silver Institute, an organization based in Washington that primarily represents silver producers. The other large lobbying organization of the silver industry is the Silver Users Association. It logs consumption of the silver mined by the companies that supply the production information to the Silver Institute.

In addition to the fundamental approach to silver price guesstimates, many traders resort to the technical approach. In this approach the trader uses prepared charts or he may prepare his own charts based on certain premises that will signal when to buy or sell or where the price of silver may go to if certain patterns on the chart occur.

A third method, growing in popularity, is the econometric or statistical approach to research.

In this method a computer is programmed with known variables and formulae in order to produce buy and sell points based on regressions.

Some traders have resorted to using cyclic systems and wave systems to bolster their decisions to enter or exit a market, to go long or go short, or to resort to another intelligent aspect of futures trading by simply standing aside (doing nothing). Probably the best advice anyone can ever give a trader is "when in doubt do nothing."

Writing this book has been a rather traumatic experience because of attempting to make a highly complex subject clear. If it contributes to the understanding of the risks and rewards of trading in silver, then the effort will have been worthwhile. Should you be interested in learning about silver trading, including its risks and rewards, I shouldn't be too hard to find in the Manhattan phone book.
Good luck!

*

GLOSSARY

ACTUALS. See PHYSICALS.

ARBITRAGER. A trader who buys in one market, and simultaneously sells in another market, the same commodity.

ACCOUNT EXECUTIVE. A commissioned or salaried person who services futures trading accounts.

BULLION DEALER. A firm whose main source of income comes from buying and selling physical precious metals.

BUTTERFLY. A spread involving longs in two differing months and shorts in other month or months on the same exchange in silver futures. Usually the form of the butterfly would be long a September and March silver and short two Decembers, etc.

BUY HEDGE. A user enters the futures market and goes long to protect his firm in case of a subsequent price rise in the underlying commodity.

CALL. A commodity option giving the holder the right to call away from the account of the grantor a specific lot of a commodity, such as silver, at an agreed price by an agreed date. The holder can never lose more than the fee or cost (premium plus commission) of the call no matter how far down the market goes during the life of the call, nor is the holder compelled to accept the delivery of the underlying commodity if the price is unfavorable.

CFTC. Acronym for the Commodity Futures Trading Commission.

COIN BAGS. Canvas bags containing $1,000 face value of dimes, quarters, or half dollars struck before 1965. The New York Mercantile Exchange lists for trading coin bag futures contracts covering lots of ten bags each.

COINS. In this book the term covers silver coins such as those involved in coin bags, and mention is made of collector coins, such as the 1801 silver dollar that sold for $525,000 in 1980.

CLEARINGHOUSE. The appendage of a commodity future exchange that issues and cancels contracts to buy and/or to sell on that exchange and collects margins and pays out margins to clearing members of the involved exchange.

CLEARING MEMBER. A member of a commodity futures exchange who has met the financial requirements of the exchange for such a designation and who has deposited the necessary bonds or treasury bills required by the clearinghouse for such exchange membership. Accounts of clearing members are settled every day via the clearinghouse.

COMMERCIAL. Refers to an exchange member or account of a member who trades in futures contracts primarily for hedging purposes rather than speculation. Orders entered on the floor by members for a commercial account are for that account as principal.

COMMISSION HOUSE. Refers to such firms as Conti, Bache, Merrill Lynch, etc. whose main business is acting as agents for customers, speculators and hedgers.

COMMODITY OPTION. See CALL.

CONGESTION. When the open interest in a specific month on a futures exchange has been concentrated in the hands of only a few longs who may intend to take delivery and thereby "squeeze" the shorts who hold the opposite side of the long contracts, but may not be in a position to make delivery to the longs. Oddly enough, congestion refers only to the long side of the open interest and not to the short side.

CORNER. Such a situation occurs when the holders of the long futures intend to take delivery knowing there are no ready supplies of the underlying commodity for the shorts to be able to make delivery. In such a case, the shorts have to "settle up" with the longs by paying plenty. The last successful silver corner was in the eighteenth century.

DAILY TRADING LIMIT. The amount by which a future contract can be settled on the exchange higher than or lower than the previous day's settlement. When silver went from 20 cents daily limit to $1 per ounce limits, its volatility had expanded by 500 percent.

DEFICIT. When an account has used up its equity and the market price is such that the positions if liquidated would leave a loss in the account—without any funds or collateral—the account is said to be in deficit. Upon liquidation, if the customer doesn't come up with the money, the deficit is charged to the account executive until the member firm recovers legally from the customer.

DELIVERY. The holder of a short contract in silver promises to make delivery of 5,000 ounces of silver in 1,000-ounce bars of a grade and brand acceptable to the exchange. The seller can deliver the silver to the long at any time during the delivery month, that is, up to and including the last delivery day set by the exchange.

DELIVERY MONTH. See SPOT MONTH.

EFP. An acronym representing *exchange for physicals*. In this case the holder of the long side of the open interest and the holder of the short side of the open interest can liquidate their obligations and reduce their exposures by actually making and taking delivery of the involved silver, whether the silver is of exchange delivery grade or not. Naturally, if subgrade silver is delivered by the short in such a case the long might be compensated accordingly.

EQUITY. The amount of money a futures trader would receive if the involved account were liquidated at the settlement price. Thus, if an account had $20,000 in cash and nothing else at the commission house, his equity would be $20,000. If a contract of March silver were purchased the following day at $16 an ounce and during the session the silver rose to $16.20 and settled at that price, the account would have gained an increase in equity of 20 cents per ounce, or $1,000. If silver had declined instead of appreciated by a similar amount, the account's equity would have dropped by $1,000, etc.

EQUITY MARGIN. See MAINTENANCE MARGIN.

EXCHANGE FOR PHYSICALS. See EFP.

EXECUTION. The state of a buy or sell order of commodity futures that has been successfully traded in the pits.

FCM. Acronym for Futures Commission Merchant. See COMMISSION HOUSE.

FIRST NOTICE DAY. The first day a short can tender the physical commodity involved in a futures contract to a long who hasn't liquidated by offset. In brief, it is actually the first day of a spot month, even though it may come in the last week of a previous month.

FOREIGN INVESTORS. A term applied to speculators who are not American citizens.

FORWARD DELIVERY. A term usually applied to metals sold for future delivery on the London Metal Exchange. There the term means precisely three months from the date of the trade if it doesn't fall on a weekend or national holiday.

FULLY HEDGED. A condition where a metals user or producer takes action in the futures markets (long or short) in the amount precisely covering the physicals to be purchased or delivered. Thus, if a mine intends to deliver 5 million silver ounces in six months to the market, it would normally go short an equivalent number of silver contracts on Comex or CBOT. If it sold short only 2.5 million ounces, it would be half-hedged, or underhedged. If it sold 10 million ounces for the same delivery month, but only intended to deliver 5 million, it would be overhedged, or speculating with 5 million ounces, etc.

FUTURES ACCOUNT. A customer account at a registered FCM (commission house involving the purchase and sale of futures contracts).

FUTURES EXCHANGES. All exchanges in the United States that have trading areas for the purchase and sale of futures contracts between members.

FUTURES MARGIN. The amount of money required by the FCM from any speculator or hedger to guarantee the soundness of the contract made on behalf of that customer. Unlike trades in securities, where there is a creditor/debtor relationship between broker and customer, the money required for futures margins is merely a guarantee of the good faith of the parties to the contract.

GOLD FIX. An event that occurs twice a day in London, England (once in the morning and once in the afternoon) at the office of N. M. Rothschild & Sons. Five members of the London Gold Market meet at these sessions to reach a mutually agreeable price, called a "fixing" or "fix."

GOLD/SILVER RATIO. A yardstick that has persevered over the ages since biblical times. It reflects how many ounces of silver it would take to purchase one ounce of gold. If the ratio is very high, it signifies that gold may be overpriced in comparison to silver. If the ratio is too low, the reverse may be true. For about a hundred years the gold/silver ratio has averaged 32/1.

HEDGE. An opposite contract in a commodity future to the physical commodity expected to be purchased or sold. Thus, a user of silver, in order to protect against price increases, would make a *buy hedge* by going long silver; a producer, in order to protect against a future decline in price, would go short silver. This is called a *sell hedge.*

INGOT. A standard silver bar weighing in the neighborhood of 1,000 troy ounces is actually an ingot. But for sales purposes, one ounce silver stampings are termed "ingots," a misnomer, of course.

INITIAL MARGIN. The good faith money required from a customer by the FCM who initiates a trade on the customer's behalf, also called *original margin.* Initial minimum margin is set by the involved futures exchange, but the member firm servicing customers may demand more if they so desire.

INTERMARKET SPREAD. A purchase and simultaneous sale of silver either for the same months or differing delivery months on more than one exchange.

INTRAMARKET SPREAD. A purchase and simultaneous sale of silver for differing delivery months on the same exchange.

INTERPRODUCT SPREAD. A purchase of silver futures and simultaneous sale of silver coin bags, or vice versa.

INTERRELATED SPREAD. Purchase of a gold future and simultaneous sale of a silver future for same or differing delivery months, and vice versa.

LEVERAGE CONTRACTS. In the sense that they are sold over the phone with limited risk provisions, leverage contracts are simply option substitutes. See CALL.

LIQUIDATION. When a long or a short in futures wants to end risk and close out the involved trade, the long sells and/or the short buys a futures contract opposite to the existing position, and the position thereby is offset by liquidation. The differential between the liquidating exit price and the original entry price when the long or short originally was established is a profit or loss.

LME. Acronym for London Metal Exchange, founded 1877.

LOCAL. An exchange member who basically trades for his or her own account. Some locals also execute orders for other members by acting as "floor brokers."

LONG. A speculator or hedger who assumes the price of a futures contract will rise and make a buy contract. A long is also called a bull.

MANIPULATION. The complex process of attempting to drive the price of silver up. Most market-watchers attribute such a ploy to the longs. But in the case of silver, the manipulation came from the shorts.

MARK-TO-THE-MARKET. When a trader or option grantor is on the wrong side of the market, he or she is required to deposit on a daily basis dollar-for-dollar the amount of money occasioned by the market adverse price change.

MAINTENANCE MARGIN. After an account has deposited the initial margin required by the FCM to execute a trade, the equity position of that account changes according to the action in the market. If an account is short silver in a rising market he would be required to add more money to maintain the position. This is called "variation" margin. If the account were long silver and the price declined, he would be called on to add more money to maintain the equity. This equity margin is also called maintenance margin.

NOTICE. The actual issuance of a piece of paper signifying a *tender*.

OPEN INTEREST. An open long position and a corresponding short position in a futures contract month add up to only one open interest. Thus the sum of the longs and the shorts divided by two equals the open interest.

OPTIONS. Contracts to buy or to sell specific amounts of physical silver at a fixed price and by a preset date. The buyer of an option who seeks to simulate a long position purchases a call; and the buyer of an option who seeks to simulate a short position buys a put.

ORIGINAL MARGIN. See INITIAL MARGIN.

PAPER TRADING. A riskless method of trading silver futures or any other futures. The paper trader uses mind-money instead of real money and trains himself or herself to watch markets and make trading decisions, etc.

OVERHEDGED. A condition where a hedger has positioned more futures contracts than required to protect the hedger against price risks. Therefore, overhedged is simply a speculative position over the hedging requirements. See FULLY HEDGED.

PHYSICALS. Futures contracts in silver involve physical silver bars of a certain fineness and weight. The silver bars tendered for delivery or stored in warehouses are known as "physicals" or "actuals."

POSITION. Most futures transactions rarely last longer than a few days. A purchase or sale of silver in any delivery month establishes a "position" for the involved account. If the position is carried on the books for more than a day, it is an open position and can be closed at any time before the delivery month by liquidation via offsetting contract purchase or sale.

POSITION LIMITS. Dictated for speculators, these limits preclude the possibility of any speculator or group of speculators acting in concert of creating a squeeze or corner on the shorts. Position limits in silver were specifically created to make the longs liquidate their holdings. The limits were enacted by the directors of the involved silver exchanges.

POSITION TRADER. A trader who is not seeking short-term, in-and-out small profits or losses, but instead accumulates contracts hoping to profit from the major trend.

PROMPT DATE. Settlement date for all LME contracts. No money or physicals change hands until the prompt date.

PUBLIC OUTCRY. The method used to buy and sell futures contracts in the silver pits. There are exceptions, such as EFP transactions, but, outside of exceptions, all trades on the exchange floor occur by public outcry, a synonym for screaming.

REPORT. Refers to transmission of information concerning an order that has been executed. Thus report is synonymous with EXECUTION.

RETENDER. The process of offering silver that has been tendered to a certain long to another clearing member customer.

RING TRADING MEMBER. An LME member who has ring-trading privileges. Currently there are about fifteen such exalted personages.

ROLL OVER. The process of moving forward a futures position that nears the spot month. The old position is liquidated and simultaneously reestablished for a farther-out delivery month.

SELL HEDGE. A producer goes short futures contracts to protect the price of the product being produced.

SHORT. A risk-taker who decides the price of silver is too high and desires to profit by a decline. The opposite of a LONG.

SILVER FIX. An event that occurs in London each trading day after the morning gold fix. Three members of the London Gold Market assemble in the office of Mocatta & Goldsmid and fix the silver price there. Since silver trades on the LME and gold does not, the gold fix is more important to the world than the silver fix. Most traders eye the fix and then watch what happens on the LME.

SILVER PHYSICALS. See PHYSICALS.

SILVER PIT. Trading area on an exchange floor where silver futures contracts are negotiated by public outcry.

SILVER RULE 7. A rule enacted by the Comex Board in January 1980 setting position limits that stifled the amount of contracts any speculator could hold in position. Subsequent effect compelled the longs to reduce their holdings substantially.

Glossary

SILVER SHARES. Securities in publicly held corporations whose main business involve silver production or processing.

SILVER SPREADS. See INTERMARKET, INTRAMARKET, INTERPRODUCT, and INTERRELATED SPREADS. Also see BUTTERFLY.

SPECULATION. A risk-taker in futures who is not going long or short in the market to protect positions in physicals is a speculator. Hedgers who overhedge are also speculators. The buy and sell orders entered into the marketplace by silver speculators are called "spec orders," or speculation. Unlike stock exchange sentiment, speculation is a healthy ingredient in the futures markets because it permits bona fide hedgers to shift their risk. If there were no speculation, there would be no futures industry or markets.

SPOT MARKET. Equivalent of cash market.

SPOT MONTH. The nearest traded month in a futures contract; usually can trade without limits either up or down.

SQUEEZE. When longs have open contracts in excess of the shorts' ability to find deliverable grade silver, the market is said to be "squeezed." A squeeze, obviously, can happen only to shorts.

SWITCH. A maneuver where the holder of a long or short futures contract in a specific delivery month offsets that position and simultaneously switches to another month, usually the spot month. When silver went limit-down day after day, holders of the far-out months who wanted to exit their risk "switched" to the limitless spot month and took a beating just to get out of the market.

TENDER. A "notice" is served on the clearing member acting for a long by the short clearing broker signifying that the short is going to deliver the silver involved. If the long has been served a tender, he can escape delivery by making a "retender."

THE TRADE. Means the bullion dealers.

TRADE HOUSE. Means a bullion dealer or metals dealer.

TRADE THE TREND. Make in-and-out trades in the market according to market direction of the major trend.

TRADING LIMITS. The amount the price of a future can vary above or below the settlement price of the previous day. Trading limits have always been set by the involved futures exchange.

TRADING PLAN. What every good account executive prepares and follows, making appropriate changes according to conditions in the market.

TRIPLE NINE SILVER. 99.9 percent pure silver.

UNDERHEDGE. A condition where the hedger puts on less contracts than required to provide price protection. See FULLY HEDGED.

VARIATION MARGIN. The daily adverse action in the market to the position of a short. This margin is required to protect the soundness of the clearinghouse and assure that the short will either liquidate or make delivery when required.

WHIPSAW LOSSES. Going long just before the market drops and then selling out at a loss and going short, only to find the market has reversed and now the short position is losing money.

*

INDEX

195